EXECUTIVE FUNCTIONING SUPERPOWERS

INCLUSIVE STRATEGIES THAT EMBRACE NEURODIVERSITY
AT HOME AND IN THE CLASSROOM. HELPING KIDS STAY
CALM, GET ORGANIZED AND ACHIEVE SUCCESS.

MÁIRE POWELL

MAIREPOWELL.COM

Illustrations by Mads Johan Øgaard

Illustrator & Special Education teacher

madsjohanogaard@gmail.com

madsjohanogaard.com

I would like to dedicate this book to my mother, Cora Powell, who passed away before its publication. Her unwavering love and support were a constant source of inspiration for me, and I am forever grateful for the guidance and encouragement she provided throughout my life.

The ripples of your love and kindness to all will be felt for generations.

Enjoy the fruits of your labor.

Train up a child in the way he should go; even when he is old he will not depart from it.

— PROVERBS 22:6

CONTENTS

INTRODUCTION

Executive functioning is not about knowing things. It's about using what you know for effective performance in life—for social, occupational, and educational effectiveness.

— RUSSELL BARKLEY, PH.D.

We all know that superheroes have incredible superpowers. But it takes time to learn how to master their skills and acquire new ones. For example, Bruce Wayne (a.k.a. Batman) had to travel around the world to look for teachers who could help him master his crime-fighting skills. By using this book, you will learn everything necessary to help your child develop their own executive functioning superpowers so that they can succeed not only in learning but also in life.

It's quite likely that nobody understands frustration like a child with executive functioning delays. In their minds, everything seems to come so easily for their peers; it can feel like the entire world is designed in a foreign way. That's because many of these children are 'neurodiverse.' Neurodiverse is a term that simply means that the brain develops, processes, learns, and behaves differently in comparison to another person whose brain works more typically. Sometimes there are significant differences. These differences can also be minute and may go unnoticed into adulthood. Scientists now understand that neurodiversity has its benefits, and people who think a little differently are able to offer unique perspectives.

Let's look at an average school day in the life of Timmy, an intelligent, happy, and curious sixth grader. He settles into his desk in English class and begins fumbling in his backpack for the homework assignment he spent so much time on last night. He wants to scream when he realizes his mistake. This morning, he ran inside to get his soccer cleats that he had forgotten. In his search, he put the English binder next to the door and forgot to grab it in his rush to the bus. The teacher is disappointed because she thought he had been making progress. She doesn't quite believe another story of completed homework left at the door, so she chastises him.

Lunch and recess are by far Timmy's favorite parts of the day. He has always been a social, kind, and funny boy who makes friends easily. But lately, it seems many of his old friends are pulling away from him. Timmy is very loud and rambunctious, rarely sitting still and constantly interrupting. An old friend said some hurtful things when he kept talking about his new video game for the third time this week. Their words hurt Timmy's feelings deeply, but he is also sorry for annoying his friends. He doesn't want to pester them; it's just so exasperating that he doesn't know what he's doing wrong or how to rectify the situation.

School's out, and it's finally time for soccer! He's quite a good player with loads of endurance, but he has never been one of the starting players. Today he was so focused on getting the ball that he ended up running in the wrong direction and kicked the ball into his own team's goal! Needless to say, his coach and teammates were not too pleased with that performance.

By the time he arrives home, Timmy just wants to watch TV until it's time for dinner. His mom asks him and his little sister to set the table, but he doesn't do his part. When his sister tattles on him, he yells at her and says hurtful things. After dinner, he is sent straight to his room to do his homework.

Stories like this are far too common. Poor Timmy tried his hardest and truly put his best foot forward every step of the way, but it just wasn't enough. He still experienced problem after problem from morning until night. Children like Timmy often slip through the cracks because many kids who have problems with executive functioning skills often seem pretty average, although maybe a little scatterbrained. Although these children can actually be very bright, they often struggle academically because of how important these skills are in every aspect of life.

It's a struggle to raise a child who has so much difficulty with seemingly simple tasks. Parents and teachers sometimes label them as lazy or troublesome early on because it's hard to see another explanation for why they cannot accomplish a mundane chore like taking out the trash. It's important to note that they do not always choose to act this way, and a parent showing excessive frustration is not likely to help the situation. These children have not developed the skills necessary to plan, solve problems, or control impulses— three things that are imperative for academic success and a peaceful home life. It's difficult to know how to act at times because the normal tricks employed to get kids involved do not work. Because of this, many parents can be inconsistent with their parenting methods, wavering between wanting to cater to the needs of their child and knowing they need to learn independence.

Many, if not most, neurodiverse children will have trouble with some executive functioning skills during their childhood. Everyone has a different style of learning, and while neurodiverse kids need a little extra attention or a different approach, they **can** master these skills. The neurodiversity movement that has been gaining momentum since the 1990s has made great strides in increasing acceptance of those who think and learn a bit differently. People with autism, attention deficit hyperactivity disorder (ADHD), or other learning differences are just as able as anyone else once their learning style is understood and a program is put in place. Classrooms and workplaces have been greatly improved by the increased participation of those with a different way of approaching life.

The truth of the matter is that to solve the problem, there will be a mixture of being a helping hand in a lot of different ways and allowing them to fend for themselves. This book is a must-read for parents and teachers who have kids that are struggling with activities that require independence and complex actions. You will discover how to rewire your child's brain in a way that makes some of these concepts finally click. Learn about effective techniques, tips, and games that are trusted by parents, educators, and therapists alike to get kids excited about the process.

The personal involvement of the child is pertinent to the success of any successful application of resources and strategies. This book will delve into the mental workings of children with executive functioning delays to gain a better understanding of where they are and how to get them on board. Once the source of the problem is understood by using the methods and resources shared in this book, the possibilities that exist will seem endless. Sometimes, executive functioning delays coexist with other disorders or require a bit more help and consistency between home and school. This book supports the reader as they guide neurodiverse learners in overcoming executive functioning challenges on a practical level, thus bridging the gap between home and school.

IS IT JUST A PHASE?

It's common for parents to feel worried or apprehensive about their child's development. Competition is pretty tight as it is in the working world: it's normal to feel worried about your child's place in the world that will exist for them. The modern world is a bustling place; it can be difficult even for adults to navigate at times. As more technology is added to day-to-day life, the way we interact with the environment is altered as well. The same is true for our children, and this makes it hard to decipher what's normal and what's not normal at times. It's so important to ensure the youngest generation learn the skills necessary to live a life of contentment, but with the world changing so rapidly, it takes some discernment to determine what exactly is age-appropriate behavior for young children.

There is no denying that much is asked of children in the 21st century, both socially and academically. It's so important to take in the big-picture when considering whether a kid has an executive functioning disorder or if they're simply overstressed. For example, if forgetting to complete homework assignments is a long-standing issue, it's important to consider other factors that may impact the student's ability to complete their assignments. How much homework is assigned nightly, for all classes combined? Between extra-curricular activities, traveling from place to place, eating, and sleeping, is there enough time to complete the work? Extra-curricular activities are an important part of a well-rounded education, but the amount of time required to participate in such activities may have been underestimated in the past. A child who participates in just one sport will likely not return home until dinner. This doesn't leave much time for homework, and often no time to decompress. Lately, there has been some pushback on excessive homework assignments, which makes sense given the present length of the school day. Many schools are changing how homework is assigned —like only allowing work to be sent home in one subject per day— while some schools are scrapping the idea of homework altogether.

Typically, a deficiency in this area will manifest in more than just a lack of homework completion. These skills are broad, encompassing all areas of life and building upon one another in added layers of complexity. Some common traits that point to an executive functioning disorder are as follows:

- Forgetting tasks and homework.
- Trouble starting work independently.
- Difficulty estimating how long a task will take.
- Difficulty keeping track of belongings.
- Easily distracted.
- Inability to remember names and other key details.
- Trouble listening to and following instructions.
- Moving on to another task before one is finished.
- Difficulty remembering and following multi-step instructions.

- Problems understanding roles in multi-part organizations, like sports teams.
- Trouble transitioning between tasks.
- Feel overwhelmed at school.
- Trouble solving problems.

Of course, these traits exist on a spectrum and may be more or less intense due to outside factors. A pediatrician or family doctor can help parents take in the big picture and figure out what is happening. Early intervention is key, as is understanding and open communication. Executive functioning skills are necessary for children to have a good life, and the reasons *why* should be stressed. Give them the motivation to work on themselves by pointing out all of the things that could be improved. Always remember, however, that they really cannot help the way they are. Some people, for some reason or another, have trouble learning these skills and often lag a bit behind their peers no matter what type of personal work they do. It's important that the child understands that they are not lazy or unintelligent.

Executive dysfunction is not usually recognized as such until around middle school. This is the time when their schoolwork and personal care should be performed independently for the most part, so any problems will likely become apparent at this time. The reason why—in the absence of other disabilities or disorders—executive delays are not diagnosed or treated in young children is because there is a lot of overlap in the behaviors of executive delayed kids and toddlers. That is, in fact, an easily recognized sign that there needs to be some work done to correct the behavior. Even so, many parents say that, looking back, there were signs of an issue early on. In the toddler years, perhaps the major warning sign is not so much that a behavior occurs, but instead, how often and how severe the instances of that behavior are. Excessive trouble in the following areas may indicate future difficulty in executive functioning skills:

- trouble taking turns
- trouble following directions with multiple steps
- inattention
- impatient
- problems with change
- temper tantrums

Early understanding of the child's needs can make a huge difference. Executive functioning skills build on one another, so problems that are corrected at a young age will be much easier for everyone involved. However, it's important not to become stressed over the matter. Young kids will exhibit such signs from time to time simply because they are young and don't know any better.

WHAT IS EXECUTIVE FUNCTION?

Before understanding whether there is any sort of dysfunction, it first needs to be understood what "executive function" is. Executive functions are the skills or traits used in daily life that help in accomplishing necessary and often complex tasks. Those with high levels of executive functioning will use whatever skills they have with the most efficiency. Problem solving, working memory, time management, and organization are all important traits that facilitate success in an educational or working environment. Skills like flexibility, impulse control, emotional regulation, and self-monitoring assist with interacting with the environment in a positive manner. Those with high levels of emotional function are more likely to experience success in school, work, and health.

Executive functions develop one after another in life. This occurs from around age two and is fully completed by around 30 years old. The seven main executive functions are adaptable thinking, self-monitoring, organization, planning, time-management, working memory, and self-control. Most children with ADHD—up to 90%, in fact—experience delays in acquiring and using executive functioning skills (Rosen, 2022). Although not every child with executive functioning delays has ADHD, most children with ADHD have executive dysfunction.

In early childhood, it's easy to brush off certain expectations due to young age and inexperience, but by middle school, such delays become glaringly obvious and troublesome. Executive functioning difficulties encompass more than just inattention and possible excitability or tantrums. A child who needs help and support learning these skills will seem unable to start projects, much less follow through to completion. It's not that the child is lazy or inept; in fact, many such children are just the opposite. For a variety of reasons, executive functioning skills don't develop properly in the absence of outside support.

Executive functioning skills are used in every aspect of life. By controlling oneself properly, the most control of any given situation is obtained. A sense of inhibition allows one to edit what they really think before speaking or acting out. The ability to cooperate well with peers can turn an average athlete into a soccer star, while a remarkable player doesn't do so well in the game. Shifting or transitioning between ideas, people, places, and actions is becoming more important in this fast-paced, modern world. The human family is becoming large and tight-knit. Soon, Earth's population will reach eight billion inhabitants. Having a sense of perspective and emotional regulation is paramount in community interactions.

There is so much involved in task management, and it's an important skill to begin developing in early childhood. Children love having a sense of freedom and autonomy. Assisting them in learning relevant traits is perhaps the best gift that can be given. Simply initiating a task can be a daunting thought for some. Working memory is the ability to remember multiple steps and necessary information.

If life is an orchestra, then executive function is the conductor. So many lovely instruments, with no way to control the tempo, tone, or volume, will have everyone in the vicinity running for the hills. Life is beautiful, but when it simply 'happens' to a person, the results are rarely good.

HOW EXECUTIVE FUNCTIONING SKILLS DEVELOP

There's a general consensus that everyone is born with a certain predisposition to develop traits related to executive functioning. That's not to say that someone without a tendency toward these behaviors won't be able to learn them, but they will have to work at it a little harder, at least for a while. Environmental learning and play throughout the first two years of life initiate the development of executive functioning. Social play and taking on more responsibilities at home and at school allows adults to model desired behavior and offer positive reinforcement.

Throughout childhood, the surrounding adults build an environment made to support the development of these skills, then begin to disassemble those supports as the child enters the teenage years. Of course, nobody expects perfection and mistakes will be made, but those with good executive functioning traits will continue doing well at school and at home. It's important to begin the process of removing some of the support mechanisms in the early teen years.

This gives ample opportunity for sorting out any major or frequent mistakes.

The following chart shows various executive functioning skills, as well as *how* the child should be performing each skill throughout their childhood and teenage years. Like stair-steps, each executive function grows over the years, building on what was previously learned. Any deficiency should be corrected in a timely manner to give the child the best chance at success. If there are any concerns, a chat with your child's pediatrician or teacher can help determine what, if any, steps are needed to amend the behavior.

0-24 MONTHS	2-4 YEARS	5-12 YEARS	13-18 YEARS	18+ YEARS
PLANNING				
-Watch objects and people -Grabbing -Learning to crawl, walk and eat	-Understands simple instructions -Gets a snack when hungry -Set up simple games	-Follows a plan to achieve a goal -Plays fast-paced games	-Plans social activities with peers	-Maintains different plans at one time -Establishes and meets long terms goals
TIME MANAGEMENT				
-Learning the order things happen like diaper changes, bath, and bedtime	-Waiting -Understands the seasons of the year	-Can estimate how long a task will take	-Adjusts working speed to fit time estimate	-Starts and implements systems to use time more efficiently
TASK INITIATION				
	-Starts and completes tasks that take up to 10 mins	-Starts and completes tasks that last up to an hour	-Starts tasks that take up to 90 mins to complete	-Completes tasks despite adverse conditions
ORGANISATION				
-Interested in colour, size and shape	-Understands patterns and functions -Can clean up with adult help.	-Can follow simple to-do lists -Gathers supplies for familiar outings	-Can follow more complex instructions	-Can plan and gather supplies for unfamiliar activities
PROBLEM SOLVING				
-Learns basic cause and effect by simple body movements and play	-Decision making and taking turns in play -Climbing over the baby gate	-Identifies problems, brainstorms solutions	-Can make decisions about complex problems	-Creates new solutions to ongoing issues

Executive Functioning Chart

0-24 MONTHS	2-4 YEARS	5-12 YEARS	13-18 YEARS	18+ YEARS
EMOTIONAL CONTROL				
	-May have tantrums	-Learns to control tantrums	-Experience adult emotions but may not be able to process them without help	-Manages frustrations in healthy ways
IMPULSE CONTROL				
	-Learns not to touch a hot stove	-Follows most behavioural and social norms	-May begin to exhibit risk taking behaviour	-Manages impulsive behaviour in most settings
ATTENTIONAL CONTROL				
-Imitation	-Responds to adult cues	-Able to develop planning and organisational skills that help them remain attentive	-Become more mindful of possible distractions, but may require guidance	-Reduces distraction when necessary
SELF MONITORING				
-Interested in mirrors	-Plays with other children Connects behaviour with emotion	-Checks own schoolwork for errors	-Use tools or devices to monitor performance	-Compares their behaviour to that of others

It's important for parents to consider the development of executive skills as their child gets older. Know what's normal behavior and what to keep an eye on. Talking to the child's pediatrician and teachers is a good way to get a well-rounded view of how your child's development compares to others in the same age group. Usually, slight delays can be rectified quickly and easily, especially if they are noticed and corrected at an early age.

SYMPTOMS OF EXECUTIVE DYSFUNCTION IN YOUR CHILD

Executive function disorder is not recognized as a specific condition in the DSM-5. Instead, the symptoms are present in a wide array of other disorders. There are many symptoms that can occur alone or together. Someone with anxiety likely has trouble starting projects and exhibiting inappropriate social behaviors like not talking to or playing with any of the other children at the playground. Memory and attention span may be difficult functions for a person with depression to improve upon alone. Although symptoms may or may not co-occur with others, executive functioning skills are like building blocks. Many times, some skills begin to decline because of dysfunction in another. The following symptoms are present in those who experience delays in executive functioning skills:

- Trouble controlling emotions.
- Difficulty planning, organizing, starting, or completing tasks.
- Inattentive.
- Issues with short-term memory.
- Unable to multitask or switch between tasks.
- Socially inappropriate behavior.
- Doesn't seem to learn from past mistakes.
- Difficulty solving problems.
- Trouble learning new information.

The consequences of poor executive functioning skills can be severe and are noticeable in every major area of life. There is a marked decrease in success and enjoyment in life. Some commonalities among individuals lacking such skills are:

- Sub-par performance at work or school.
- Problems with personal relationships.
- Mood issues.
- Low self-esteem.
- Lack of motivation.
- Avoidance of difficult or long-term tasks.

Because these skills develop over a long period of time, it's common and completely normal for children and adolescents to struggle as they learn. Perfection is not, and never will be, the goal, but the acquisition and implementation of executive skills should continually improve. Any concerns should be discussed with the child's doctor and possibly their educators. By taking notice early on and stepping up to manage and teach these skills, a lifetime of struggle and likely discontentment can be avoided.

WHAT'S NORMAL AND NOT NORMAL?

Many of the symptoms that are present with executive function disorder exist on a spectrum. Besides, all young kids have poor executive functioning skills. The whole purpose of a controlled childhood environment is to instill this knowledge over time, learning more complex skills as the previous ones are mastered.

It's normal for a five, six, or even seven year old to have difficulty concentrating or controlling impulses around siblings. Positive reinforcement is always a preferred method of correcting behavior as a positive state of mind is always beneficial in learning. This means offering plenty of praise and rewards that are pleasing to the child. However, age-appropriate punishments need to be carried out in response to actions that could cause physical harm. If a child continues kicking their sibling after being told to stop, a time-out is often necessary so no harm comes to either party while they cool off. A general rule of thumb for time-outs is one minute per year of age.

Many children do not do well with the separation that goes along with this method of correction. With such children, a time-out chair or time-in can be beneficial. Time-ins involve the caregiver going into a calm space with the child to be with them and explain what happens while they calm down. What works best for each family will be different, and may even change on a daily basis. For example, time-ins are a proven, effective, and gentle method of correction that does not cause undue stress. While that may be the preferred method, there may be good reasons why it isn't used. Perhaps there is a younger sibling who is getting the wrong idea about time-ins. It could be easy for a toddler to misconstrue what's happening as a reward of "time with mommy" for certain bad behavior.

One thing that is certain is that weak executive skills are not a choice and cannot be *punished* in a child. Usually, the child will be just as disappointed as everyone else when they make the same mistakes yet again.

In early elementary school, poor executive functioning skills may manifest as messiness and forgetfulness. Tantrums can be extreme at times, resembling actions that would be expected from a young toddler. There also seems to be an inability to understand, much less learn, such concepts as a schedule or estimating time.

By middle-school, most children should have more impulse control; they should think things through before speaking or taking action. At this time, it's age-appropriate to expect that the child will not kick siblings and can work semi-independently on their schoolwork. Bodily autonomy—for themselves and others—is important, and often these kids don't fully understand the concept of personal space.

Problems that manifest at this time have the potential to snowball into a big problem as school begins to gain in complexity at a fast rate from here on. The transition from little kid to big kid is a huge milestone in life. Pay close attention to everything going on at this time and be there to rectify any issues immediately.

HOW EXECUTIVE FUNCTIONING CAN AFFECT YOUR CHILD AND YOUR WHOLE FAMILY

At times, it can seem like the entire family is enduring difficulties due to a child with low executive functioning skills, and that can be true. However, nobody suffers more than the child themself. It's frustrating to experience hardships when peers have a much easier time with similar tasks. Many dislike school, and it's not because they aren't social or intelligent. It's because they are not properly equipped to deal with the environment, specific pressures, and requirements. Focusing, transitioning between subjects, working independently, and even some social aspects of school are very stressful.

Even extroverted children have social troubles at school due to poor impulse control. They may struggle with taking turns or interrupting, which puts off peers from interacting with them. It's especially hard for them because they often don't fully recognize when they do something wrong.

Family life for everyone involved can become intense as seemingly simple tasks and activities become insurmountable at times. The tantrums and general misbehavior common in young children make tasks such as getting showered, dressed, and grocery shopping a day-long ordeal that ends with everyone on edge. The careers of the parents could suffer due to exhaustion and the inability to properly manage home life. Other siblings often miss out on activities that are canceled, not scheduled, or departed from early.

The extreme messiness common in early youth is especially difficult for the family. Sometimes, as soon as one area is cleaned, another two are destroyed. This can be isolating for the whole family as embarrassment over the state of the home causes the parents not to extend invitations to extended family or friends.

By middle and high school, the sheer amount of time needed to help manage their school and social calendars can leave little time to help with the assignments of other children.

It's heartbreaking to watch a child struggle, and even worse when the whole family is thrown into turmoil. Keep in mind that they can't help their delay in executive skills and don't intend to cause such stress. Parents of young children should keep an eye out for delays and intervene, if necessary. Listen to what their teachers have to say. The school and home environments are extremely different. How a child acts in one place could be completely contradictory to how they behave in another setting.

WHAT PARENTS AND CAREGIVERS SHOULD KNOW

Parents and caregivers shouldn't feel bad for missing early signs of delayed executive function. Usually, teachers are the first to take notice because they are around so many kids of the same age and see them in a different environment. Also, because these skills are developmental, occurring in a stair-step fashion, it's common for children to only begin experiencing difficulties once they are in school and begin needing more complex skills.

It's of great importance that those in the child's life understand that executive dysfunction is **not** a learning disability. Many of these children have a high level of intelligence, and much of their frustration likely comes from feeling unable to accomplish goals with that knowledge. Talk to them, explain their strengths and weaknesses, and make plans to showcase their abilities while working to improve their deficiencies. Involving them in the process makes them feel more capable and in control. Not to mention, the task of identifying the child's problem, creating and implementing a plan, and measuring results is a huge feat for anyone, especially a child with executive functioning delays. The problem itself has the potential to be a massive learning opportunity.

Of course, intense focus will be on the skills that are lacking. Success in school, work, and one's personal life depends on improvement. But don't lose sight of the fact that the child still needs ample opportunity to showcase their strengths. All of these kids have certain areas where they can focus and perform well. It's clear that such subjects play an important role in their day-to-day lives; it's likely a matter that will remain important throughout life. Self-confidence, especially amongst peers, is paramount when mastering new abilities.

2

SEE WHAT YOU'RE WORKING WITH

C hildren have different strengths and weaknesses. At times, it's difficult to tell what's normal and what's not, especially in young children. Because small issues can quickly snowball out of control, it's a good idea to involve the child's pediatrician if there is any worry that development is not normal.

There are various reasons why the parents, school administration, or pediatrician may want to have a complete battery of neurological testing performed. Inattentiveness and hyperactivity are often concerning as they affect executive functioning skills that are so vital throughout life. Learning disorders, language disorders, and mood disorders often need to be studied more closely, as well as intellectual giftedness in combination with troubles in other aspects of life. These areas of concern may exist alone, but often there is more.

Bring up concerning behavior with your pediatrician. They may want to have the child evaluated for other conditions affecting executive functioning—ADHD being the biggest culprit. Most children with an ADHD diagnosis lag behind their peers by about three years in the development of executive functioning skills (Brown, 2022). Autism, dyslexia, or oppositional defiant disorder (ODD) are other possible factors responsible for the delay. Mood disorders such as anxiety or depression, as well as instances of trauma, abuse, or brain damage, are also possible causes of executive dysfunction.

With so many possible causes, it's tough to find a solid solution on your own. Therapists and social workers are trained in how to manage such delays in various ways. The plan of attack is customized and prioritizes learning independence at a level appropriate for their current skill level. Teachers are a treasure trove of information, even from previous grades. They observe many children who learn in different ways. They can be of great assistance when determining the diagnosis, if there is to be one.

ASSESS YOUR CHILD'S NEUROLOGICAL FUNCTIONING

In the process of discerning an accurate diagnosis, there will likely be a lot of information needed by various therapists and doctors. Many behavioral checklists should be filled out by a parent or close caregiver of the child so the team will have as much information as possible. It's likely that one of the first orders of business will be to complete one or more of the following assessments, depending on your state or region and the level of difficulty the child is experiencing, for example:

- Child Behavior Checklist
- Behavior Assessment System for Children

- Essentials of Executive Function Assessment
- Executive Skills in Children and Adolescents
- Behavior Rating Inventory of Executive Function
- Cognitive Assessment System

It can be a lot of work, but the rate at which results will manifest, once a fitting plan is established, can be quite shocking. What's surprising is how quickly a once high-needs child thrives with independence and autonomy once they learn how to function in such a way.

So many parents are fearful of gaining a diagnosis of a developmental delay. Maybe they are apprehensive about the future of their child, or perhaps they don't feel confident in their own skills in raising a neurodivergent child. Such ideas couldn't be farther from the truth. Many of the most successful individuals have brains that work a bit differently. There is no reason to believe that a child who has issues with executive function, or other related diagnosis, will lead a difficult life. Avoiding proper treatment only serves to strengthen any deficiencies. There is no reason for a parent to feel inadequate. Executive skills are normally picked up along the way by children; the best anybody can do is find help and support when a problem becomes apparent. Above all, remember that the outcome of any evaluation changes nothing about your child or the person they are. All that a diagnosis means is that more resources are now available.

Often, a proper diagnosis can open all the right doors and put the child in the proper position to participate fully in life. Not only are new and positive resources available for both the caretaker and the child, but this process allows teachers, coaches, administrators, and therapists to get to know and understand the child better. It's amazing how quickly progress can be made when everyone is on the same page and following the same recommendations.

In many cases, it may be determined that a neuropsychological evaluation is necessary. This is often in response to a combination of several factors; an extensive test is sometimes required to truly understand the root of the problem. These tests will determine an assortment of information about the child. IQ, attention levels, and academic achievement are important factors, as are emotional, behavioral, and executive functioning. Visual-motor and fine-motor skills are likely to be included. Language abilities, verbal memory, and visual memory will be tested as well.

Neuropsychological Evaluations

Neurological testing is an in-depth assessment of all aspects involved in brain function. Attention, memory, problem-solving abilities, academic abilities, language skills, social-emotional functioning, and visual-spatial skills are all a part of this battery of tests. One of the major aspects of these evaluations is to get a feel for how the child performs with a task that lacks structure. This allows for a broad picture encompassing all areas of abilities and characteristics, including problem solving abilities and creativity.

The neuropsychological evaluation will be performed by a neuropsychologist, a licensed psychologist who has completed a two year neuropsychology fellowship. There are many ways to find a neuropsychologist that the family is comfortable with. The child's pediatrician should be able to offer a referral, and the insurance company can provide a list of local neuropsychologists. Google is a great way to research individual practices to find the right fit.

Some common questions parents and guardians have when interviewing neuropsychologists would be details on how they will deal with the child and family; they should be able to offer information about the structure of their sessions. It's a good idea to have them describe the evaluation in their own words. They should be able to articulate how they plan to work with the school; it's important to know if they participate in IEP meetings or have educational recommendations.

The process of the neuropsychological evaluation is very thorough, and it's important to know what to expect. The psychologist will hold separate intake sessions for both the parents or guardians and the child. The intake session for the caregivers will last about one and a half to two hours, while the session for the child will vary based on their age. The doctor will want to get information about the home, school, and family environments from both parties, as well as their strengths and weaknesses. Depending on the age of the child, they may or may not be able to answer these questions in a straightforward way. The doctor may use drawings or games to glean the necessary information. Of great interest is how the child feels every day as they interact with the people in their life.

After the intake sessions are complete, testing begins. The neuropsychological exam is an extremely thorough battery of tests; as such, it's a rather long process. It usually takes two or three days, with each testing session lasting the length of a typical school day. Some practices prefer to spread the testing out so that it takes a longer number of days, but testing is limited to three or four hour sessions. Re-evaluations may be shorter, as well as testing for older patients. Be sure to speak with the child in preparation for the evaluation. They should understand—to the best of their abilities—what to expect and how long the process will take. They will have ample opportunity for mental breaks and refreshment. The comfort of the child is at the forefront of the minds of everyone involved.

Sometimes the neuropsychologist will need to observe the child at school. Of concern during school observation is social interaction with peers, behavior with teachers, attention, following directions, working independently, and levels of anxiety. Once testing is complete, there will be a feedback session where parents will meet with the doctor to review the results and share them with the appropriate parties, with their consent. Older children, or those at a higher level of functioning, may also be present at the feedback session. Participation of the child, if at all possible, is of vital importance in this process. Those that are able to understand this process need to feel involved. The feeling of something out of their control happening to them is a huge stressor and will likely exacerbate the current issues.

Other Conditions That Could Be Causing Disorganization

It's quite common for other conditions to be interrelated with poor executive functioning skills. These conditions are recognized types of neurodivergence and include autism, ADHD, bipolar disorder, and obsessive-compulsive disorder (OCD). ADHD, however, is the most common disorder associated with disorganization. Almost all those who suffer from ADHD present with a lack of executive functioning skills and generally check off a large number of possible symptoms. Lack of attention and impulse control is generally what causes the snowball effect that eventually causes deficiencies in other skills. Someone who cannot pay attention or control themselves can't make proper plans.

Some people with autism have some sort of trouble with organization and implementation of plans. Autism has many faces, and those with autism are varied in their dispositions. The way low-levels of executive functioning are present will look different from person to person. Some have very conceptual minds but are unable to see the smaller details. Others are too focused on small details, unable to see the forest for the trees. Poor impulse control is common in those with autism, as is excessive daydreaming while neglecting to take action. Impulsive behaviors can cause disruption and distress, highlighting the need to support children in the development of skills in this area as a priority. Working memory is another component that is often difficult. Temple Grandin, a leading voice in the autism community, once said, "I cannot hold one piece of information in my mind while I manipulate the next step in the sequence" (Autism Speaks, 2022).

Obsessive Compulsive Disorder (OCD) is always associated with some sort of executive dysfunction. The hallmark of this disorder is the inability to shift attention from one specific idea or cycle to another. Multi-tasking and altering plans and schedules are important skills that are completely at odds with how OCD presents.

Bipolar disorder causes a lack of motivation and focus at times, and they usually have weak verbal memories and are less flexible than their peers. This is another disorder that isn't thought to affect kids, but it presents at about the same rate as in the adult population. This disorder can have serious consequences if not treated early.

Depression and anxiety usually go hand-in-hand with executive functioning issues. Short-term depression and anxiety troubles are usually the catalysts for a loss of these skills. In those cases, skills begin to improve as the mood lifts. Those suffering from chronic depression or anxiety need more attention to obtain acceptable levels of executive function. The exhaustion common with depression makes planning nearly impossible. On the other hand, the poor impulse control observed in some with chronic anxiety makes following through with meticulous plans a pipe dream.

Parents, educators, doctors, and therapists of children with mood or brain disorders should have a clear understanding of what executive functioning skills are and how to assist in their development. Nearly every child (and adult) with a mental condition will have trouble with at least some of the executive functioning skills. That's not to say they can't achieve as much as anyone else, but these children need a plethora of love and support in their corner to succeed.

ADVOCATE FOR YOUR CHILD

Parents can, and should be, their child's biggest cheerleader. Ensure that those involved in the child's life and education are on the same page with an understanding of exactly where they are at the present moment. It's easy for doctors, educators, and even parents to misunderstand or overlook certain behaviors because the respective environments in which they observe the child are distinctive.

Keep extensive notes on the child's behavior, including information about recent life changes or current diet if there are any abnormalities to be noted. Keep lists of any questions or concerns. Preparation before doctor's appointments or intake sessions is essential in obtaining correct and timely diagnostic information.

Take any concerns that educators and school systems have to heart. Most parents don't observe their children in such a large group for long periods of time. Behavior and actions in such an environment can differ greatly from what is normal at home. Teachers have years of experience watching all types of children interact together in such an atmosphere. They are generally accurate when they hone in on something abnormal. When all those concerned for the child's well-being are on the same page, wonderful results can be seen. Teaching executive functioning skills doesn't have to be difficult, but the overall rules must remain consistent for new habits to form.

For these children to succeed in life, their parents or caregivers must be effective and informed advocates who are tuned into their needs. If executive delays or any other disorders are suspected, be sure to take proper care of the situation by keeping the following tasks in mind:

- gather information.
- know the procedures.
- plan and prepare for meetings or evaluations with the school or in therapy.
- keep extensive written records.
- ask plenty of questions and pay keen attention to the answers.
- identify problems.
- propose possible solutions.
- determine goals and make a plan to accomplish them.
- teach the child how and where to seek help when needed.

One of the most beneficial ways to advocate for a child is to teach them how to speak up and ask for help when they don't understand something. There's often a reluctance to go to a teacher for help when they don't understand something. By middle school, concepts are becoming quite complex and it can be difficult for a child to properly vocalize what it is they need help with. Sometimes, they don't even quite know *what* needs a more detailed explanation.

FINDING SOLUTIONS

The good news is that, for the most part, executive functioning delays can be overcome. However, there are no one-size-fits-all solutions available. Every caregiver is on a unique mission to learn how to teach these life skills, and there will likely be a lot of trial and error before a viable plan begins to form. Many children will benefit greatly from nothing more than additional parental support applied in the right way and a few easy classroom accommodations. Others may require different types of treatment. like cognitive behavioral therapy, occupational therapy, or speech therapy. Sometimes, medication may be recommended for other connected conditions.

When dealing with learning, and mood issues, especially in children, nothing is static. There will be constant evaluations to check if the plan is still working successfully or what—if any—changes need to be made. Many parents are against medication but quickly come to see what a difference it can make in setting up good habits. Many people don't realize that taking medication isn't something that will necessarily continue indefinitely. Sometimes, once a few basic executive skills are learned for some stability, medication may be discontinued under the guidance of the prescribing professional. It's also pretty time consuming and confusing to see so many therapists on a regular basis. This, too, shall pass. In the beginning stages, there may be several types of therapy the child needs to take part in, but this is likely to change as improvements are made.

There's no harm in trying some teaching activities while determining the extent of the problem or waiting to meet with a medical team, and the information discussed in this book can be implemented without any sort of medical degree.

The following chapters will outline simple techniques that have been proven successful over time for treating executive dysfunction. They can be employed without supervision from a doctor or licensed therapist, although if you feel your child needs further intervention, please reach out to their pediatrician. Children tend to improve with time. In the absence of other disorders, executive functioning delays are just that—delays. Remember, skills tend to improve with age.

3

CREATING A CONDUCIVE ENVIRONMENT

Opportunities for the development and execution of critical skills should abound in the child's environment, at school, and at home. There are many hidden moments and methods that can have an impact on a child. They often don't need much of a push to really take off. Be proud as the children in your life learn new modes of behavior and leave behind some of their childish and stubborn ways. A common mistake that anyone trying to enact a change makes is forgetting about previously mastered skills and abilities. Nothing is forever, and skills that are not practiced could eventually become extinct. It's important to work on new skills *and* allow for conditions that showcase skills that have already been mastered. These children often come to understand that they lack the level of discipline and judgment seen in their peers as they age, and they crave approval and validation. Self-esteem gets a boost from having a continual rate of success, so ensure that they are set up for favorable outcomes at regular intervals.

Three brain functions are involved in the regulation of executive function. Mental flexibility, working memory, and self-control work in concert to determine an individual's level of executive function. Mental flexibility is the ability to multitask or shift between constantly changing environmental demands. Some settings require different rules; mental flexibility is important in understanding *how* to change personal behavior in accordance with the surrounding location and people who are present.

Working memory is like a mental scratch pad where multiple important pieces of information are stored and easily remembered. Those with strong working memories can mentally manipulate that information and estimate what the outcome will be.

Self-control is all about delayed gratification. There are a certain set of actions that must be performed to get the desired outcome. Although many of those steps are not desirable, self-control is what makes people stick it out until the end. By creating an environment ripe with opportunity to develop these three brain functions, the child will be given the best start in life.

LAYING THE FOUNDATION

Although some children have a tendency towards higher levels of executive function, everyone needs to be taught these critical skills. Some children just require a bit more help along the way. It's essential that parents, caregivers, and teachers do what they can to make the environments they control conducive to promoting executive functioning skills. Understand your child's personality and experiment with different methods to find what works best for them.

Although it doesn't seem like it at the time, childhood passes extremely quickly. The young adults who are best prepared to enter the world will have had plenty of structured opportunities to make the right decisions. This is done through various methods, such as modeling acceptable behavior, scaffolding, and setting a routine. Children learn from repetitive behaviors, so any action a parent wants from them needs to be practiced on a continual basis.

Social connections are paramount throughout early childhood and adolescence. Activities that foster social connections will change with age. While it's necessary for children to step out of their comfort zones from time to time, it's best when most social activities for executive delayed children take place in comfortable environments and showcase the child's strengths. Truly, this is a fair train of thought since most of their day-to-day, consists of doing things that are a struggle, like remembering all of the rules of a game or taking turns.

There should always be ample opportunity for exercise. So many children who experience delays with executive functioning also have a diagnosis of ADHD and need to drain excess energy on a regular basis.

Relationships

Over the years, multiple studies continue to show how interconnected social relationships are with executive functioning skills. It makes sense that so many of those traits are required to maintain successful relationships. Impulse control, time management, working memory, and planning all play a role in maintaining successful relationships. Positive social interaction is an integral part of building a successful adult, and such relationships are important to maintain throughout life as they allow continued opportunity to practice executive functioning skills.

It's important for parents and guardians to be a pillar of stability in their children's lives. They should feel loved and supported at home because high levels of stress have a negative effect on executive functioning traits. Instead, try to turn stressful situations into valuable learning experiences. When things don't go according to plan, talk through the steps and thoughts that come up in the search for a solution. There's no better teacher than watching life skills in action. Consciously raising children is often just as valuable a learning experience for the caregivers as it is for young ones.

Children with ADHD have a notoriously hard time building friendships. It's such a heartbreaking experience for their parents because those who are close to the child know how wonderful and special they are. As caregivers, there are things that can be done to help foster friendships among others in their peer group. Just be sure not to overstep any boundaries because some kids—especially teenagers—might feel embarrassed to have their parents openly interfere in their social life.

Joining a sports team is an excellent way to make friends. These children do well with physical exercise, so choose an activity that puts them in their zone. Stick around for practices and games, watching closely for their interactions with other kids. If possible, get close enough to hear some of the conversation. There may be useful insight to glean that could be shared at a later time. One thing to be aware of is that some children moms with ADHD are very competitive and can be both sore losers and bad winners. If this is a problem for your child, encourage individual sports that don't require teamwork, such as swimming, karate, or track.

If the child is agreeable, it may be possible to broker a friendship with a peer that shares some similar interests. Because they are usually a bit more immature than their chronological age, it's best to seek out playmates who are a little younger. Start out with only one-on-one play dates. Group functions can be overstimulating, which tends to worsen behavior, so be aware of their limits when deciding on a time frame for the activity.

Some heartfelt conversations can help get to the root of the problem. By discussing things that go wrong, you may be able to offer some insight into how they can improve the situation in the future. Keep an open line of communication and make the child's time with you a judgment free zone. Most of all, don't fret too much over a socially awkward teenager. They will bloom in their own time, and their tribe will begin to form around them. Many often prefer a smaller circle of friends anyway, and there's nothing wrong with that.

Activities

There is no shortage of activities to practice executive functioning skills. For such skills to become integrated, they must be practiced often. A few times a week should suffice, but if the stimulation is varied, the child may ask for family fun night to be every night! Variating the type of play is important, so steadily increase the level of difficulty as they master a skill. It's hard enough for these kids to stay on task; boredom threatens to derail any previous progress.

Many card games are wonderful exercises for many important skills, especially games where cards are organized in the hand, like *Uno* or *Gin Rummy*. Young kids often enjoy helping with the dishes. Show them how to put away clean plates and utensils while offering plenty of praise. Posting visually appealing schedules is an easy and fun way to incorporate time management skills into daily life. This teaches the child how much time is needed for certain activities, so they can better estimate time requirements as they get older.

Timers are another excellent method to use in teaching time management skills. Have the child look to the future with goal setting and planning. Have them write daily, weekly, monthly, or even yearly plans complete with the steps necessary for execution. Have their plans easily accessible and allow for time to update them as they begin working on them.

Games involving strategy, like chess and checkers, are another excellent way for children to practice planning and organizational skills. It's important to keep in mind that many of these children have a diagnosis of ADHD. There are plenty of activities that teach attention and patience in an enjoyable way. Yoga, dance, and martial arts are excellent for children of all ages. "Red light, green light" is a fun game for some of the youngest children, who are often at the age where they are in awe of cars and traffic. They are given the commands—red light, yellow light, or green light—and respond appropriately as if they are cars by stopping, walking, or running. They will not even realize how long they can listen to and follow directions with so much laughter!

Hide and seek is another great option, as is jumping rope, complete with all of the complicated variations as the child gets older. "Miss Mary Mack" and other hand clapping games are great at developing working memory as children work to remember both the song and the clapping movements at the same time. It's hard to memorize so many words, but it becomes easier when the task involves singing a catchy tune. It's common for children with low levels of executive functioning skills to require some work on self-regulation and inhibition. Simon Says, Musical Chairs, and any game that requires taking turns is sure to bring improvement.

Places

The places where a child spends their time are of the utmost importance. The area should feel—and be—safe. The home should be free of stress and excessive triggers, and school should be an enjoyable environment most of the time. If the child isn't happy or doesn't feel safe in their frequented environments, it's up to parents to investigate why and implement changes. Economic instability is a common reason why the home doesn't feel safe. Although many parents are unable to significantly improve their financial situation, they can often do things that help ease some of the tension that goes along with the stress of poverty.

All kids need the opportunity to be creative, explore, and get exercise. Art projects are a great way to get young children excited about making a plan. Perhaps a child is so excited about making a snowman out of three paper plates that they are willing to pay attention to, and remember, the directions. Start small with easy projects to build self-confidence and eventually move on to more difficult or mundane activities. Many such children have excess energy that inhibits concentration. By allowing for daily exercise, some of the brain fog clears, making way for better decision making. Before trying to make changes in the child, first see if a few minor alterations in the physical environment is beneficial.

CLASSROOM ACCOMMODATIONS

In the United States (US), children with disabilities or diverse learning styles have legal protections through the Every Student Succeeds Act and Individuals with Disabilities Education Improvement Act that ensure they are able to learn in a general education classroom. This is difficult, as there are many barriers to learning that exist for these children that do not exist—at least to the same extent—in the general population. The way the information is presented may be difficult to understand, as well as the way in which they are expected to respond. The environment of the classroom could be distracting, or the instruction takes place at a bad time of the day for their schedule. Classroom accommodations exist to help students overcome these barriers so that they have the same opportunity to receive an education as everyone else.

Please note: If you reside outside of the US, you will need to check the legislation of your country of residence.

Most accommodations fall under two categories: Instructional and testing. Essentially, the instructions are presented in a different way and the testing is performed differently, but the material taught and tested does not change. There is no unfair advantage given to children who receive classroom accommodations—as is a common misconception. Instead, they act as an equalizer between students who learn and act very differently from one another. It makes perfect sense to offer different forms of instruction to ensure nobody is left behind.

It has become common for classrooms to offer a variety of accommodations to students with various needs. As long as there is an individualized education plan (IEP), which lays out the framework for how a student is to achieve success, the school system must make arrangements. If your child doesn't have a diagnosis for a learning or developmental disability, it can be helpful to speak with teachers and school staff regarding simple changes, as they may be willing and able to make them. Executive functioning skills are an important part of the educational experience and all children benefit from such practices, even those who seem to have mastered such skills.

It has been recommended that teachers collaborate with athletic coaches on occasion. It is an interesting suggestion, but it makes sense, and teachers have seen success by taking this advice. Coaches tend to have an uncanny ability to know when their players understand a concept. They are invaluable resources as the relationships they have with the children are unique and important.

Schedules

Children should have an easily identifiable routine. Simple things, such as posting a daily schedule along with hanging an "easy to read" clock on the wall, can work wonders in keeping children on task and alleviating anxiety. Items can be checked off as they are completed, so the children can visually see the results of planning and organization.

Abrupt schedule changes could cause upset or over-excitement, so try to inform students of any deviations as soon as possible. Kids that have trouble with change should be given extra time and patience when their normal routine is thrown off. The following table is an example of a schedule that's helpful to keep on days when school is not in session.

Before 9:00am	Wake up	Wake up, eat breakfast, brush teeth, get dressed
9:00-10:00	Outdoors	Walk, backyard time, playground
10:00-11:00	Academics	Schoolwork, reading, puzzles, no electronics
11:00-12:00pm	Creativity	Drawing, legos, cooking
12:00-1:00	Lunch	
1:00-2:00	Chores	Age appropriate tasks around the home
2:00-3:00	Quiet time	Nap, reading, meditation
3:00-4:00	Academics	
4:00-5:00	Outdoors	Playground, sidewalk chalk, sports
5:00-6:00	Dinner	Eat with family and help clear the table
6:00-7:00	Bath	
7:00-8:00	Reading/tv	Downtime to watch favorite shows or do an activity of choice
8:00-9:00	Bedtime	Put on pjs, brush teeth, put dirty clothes in the hamper

Learning Environments

The learning environment should be clear of excess clutter so that it's easier for the child to focus on the assignment. Classrooms should be relatively quiet during times when concentration is required. Many find noise canceling headphones to be a helpful tool in achieving this without putting too much pressure on class-mates. There are many comfortable and discreet devices, like those offered by Calmer Kids, which can help get the child in the right state of mind for learning.

Class Policies

It's important for children to have the opportunity to respond in an appropriate manner of their choice. Many educators have found it helpful to keep a stash of small dry-erase boards so children can show their understanding, even if it is difficult to put the answer into words. There has also been success in allowing students to indicate answers to yes/no/unsure questions with their thumbs: Thumb up for yes, thumb down for no, and thumb sideways for unsure.

Often, IEPs will include the option of taking notes and performing written assignments on a digital device.

Be the Example

The number one way that children absorb information about the world is through observation. They watch those around them and their actions long before they are able to ask questions. It's so important for teachers and caregivers to model appropriate behavior so children can easily understand and emulate positive behavior.

When Giving Instructions

Instructions should be clear, concise, given in a way that's understood, and then repeated. The most successful students understand what is expected of them. Some absorb verbal directions better, others prefer written. Teachers should post written directions as they explain them verbally. This way, all students can start out with more even-footing. It's a good idea to show examples of properly completed work. It gives the students an idea of how to proceed and takes away some of the anxiety they might feel about making an embarrassing mistake in front of their peers.

Some children need frequent reminders to stay on task. Be sure to check in on easily distracted students a bit more often. They will greatly benefit from the extra help focusing, while children who stay on task independently are often distracted by frequent reminders.

A good piece of advice to remember is the rule of three. When giving instructions:

1. Make eye contact.
2. Clearly state the instructions.
3. Ask them to repeat the instructions.

Doing this puts an end to stories about not hearing anything before it even happens.

Make Learning Hands-On

Hands-on activities involve multiple sensory inputs and are more enjoyable, especially for children with excessive hyperactivity. It seems easier for their bodies to calm down when many of their senses are busy.

One memorable way to teach a lesson is to get messy! The mess is unexpected and something that isn't normally 'allowed.' Harness the power of shock and let them get their hands dirty. It's also beneficial to ensure students are shown how they will use the information in real life. Sometimes, there is a disconnect between how learning in the classroom translates into an adult career. Teachers have the ability to offer some clarity that could increase motivation.

Use of Metacognitive Language

Metacognition is the act of thinking about one's own thoughts. In a classroom setting, using metacognitive language when explaining a task will entail describing all of the thoughts one would have and actions that would be performed, from start to finish.

Before beginning an assignment, think about what is already known about a subject and how the work is to be approached. While working on it, consider if enough progress is being made or if the pace should be increased. Maybe a shortcut has become apparent since work started. After the task is completed, determine if there was a better strategy that could have been used.

The use of metacognitive language is a tried and true method for people learning a second language. This method is exceptionally successful at teaching early executive skills in the native tongue because, as adults, much of our self-talk is so second nature it may go unnoticed and wouldn't be otherwise included in the directions. It's helpful to rehearse giving instructions ahead of time so nothing is left out. Take note of every thought and action while the task is being completed. Educators who make use of this technique have an exceptional ability to reach even the most difficult students.

Scaffolding

This is the process of building a strong support system into a child's environment to set them up for success. A parent should help in setting up a homework and study plan for a child struggling in school. Work together to determine things like *where* and *when* the work should be done, how long until a break is needed, and in what order the work will be accomplished. Most children who take medication find it helpful to work on their more difficult subjects first, before the dose begins to wear off.

Offer an incentive during breaks, especially if there's a difficult project or an abnormally heavy workload. Just ensure the reward isn't something that will cause issues when it's time to return to work. Video games normally aren't a good idea to introduce as an incentive, as it's difficult for most kids to switch back to homework. Any reward that becomes problematic when it's time to get back on task should be removed from the list of incentives. This shows consequences and helps develop accountability.

The goal of scaffolding is for the child to eventually gain independence. Over time, they take on more and more control of a task until they are able to eventually complete the process unsupervised.

Modify Tasks to Match Work Capacity

Testing methods may need to be altered so that a child's true abilities can be determined. Consider different approaches to the written portions of an exam. It is important that the student participates in such portions, but it can make a huge difference in their attitude if poor writers are given the opportunity to answer verbally and have that taken into account when the assignment is graded. When it's known that a student struggles with writing, it is unfair for them to receive lower marks for that deficiency in an unrelated subject.

Sometimes, it is in the child's best interest to receive shortened assignments as long as the same standards of learning are present as those found in the standard assignment. Oftentimes, when easily distracted kids complete certain types of work, especially tedious and repetitive assignments, the quality of their work begins to suffer as they continue working on the same types of problems. Additional time to take tests or complete assignments may be needed. Teachers should check on students who need extended time often to ensure they stay on track, especially for long-term projects.

. . .

Break Down Tasks

Young children, even those with high levels of executive function, benefit from having complex tasks broken down into smaller steps. This is likely commonplace in many learning environments during most of elementary school, but an IEP can ensure a child continues receiving help understanding how to decipher tasks requiring multiple steps. Some tips for breaking up large assignments are to:

- Select a starting point.
- Focus on problem areas.
- Build in breaks.
- Cover up all parts of the page except one particular question.
- Laminate a checklist for complex tasks that will be assigned frequently, like book reports or math equations.
- Write instructions on stacked index cards instead of a bulleted list.
- Shrink the focus of the question.
- Make connections to previously learned material.

Use of Incentives to Augment Instruction

Some children are not very easily motivated, and some tasks do not have built-in rewards. An incentive system that gives something back for appropriate behavior is necessary for some children, at least at first. Every child is different regarding what works as an incentive. Some are happy with praise, while others may learn better with a point system where they can 'earn' a desired reward. Some people don't agree with giving rewards for doing the bare minimum, but at times, the minimum is the best a child can do.

A parent who teaches a middle-schooler to do laundry may explain what to do thoroughly, organize the laundry room so supplies are easy to find, and supervise the first few loads before leaving the child alone to their own devices. That may work for children who develop executive functioning skills in a typical manner, but in other cases, the child will very quickly lose motivation, forget how to perform the task and revert back to old behavior.

It's helpful for parents to offer some sort of reward. Perhaps they could come to an agreement that if three loads of laundry are completed this week, there will be a reward of a trip to a favorite restaurant. Working towards a short-term reward makes it more pleasant to keep up with the responsibility, and the consistency in performing the task will make it easier to do over time. This also teaches the important concept of delayed gratification. After a while, it would be a good idea to select a bigger reward that is given after the laundry is done three times a week for an entire month. The process of removing the supports is just as delicate as setting them up in the first place. The best results will be seen with a slow, steady, and deliberate transformation into autonomy.

Intentionally Teach Deficient Skills

It's not uncommon for children exhibiting low executive functioning skills to be mislabeled at school and even among their own families. Some are known as "the bad kid," "the daydreamer," or "the awkward bag of nerves." Instead of labeling troubled kids, parents and teachers should look closely at the behavior they want to change and assume the child doesn't understand how to act in such a way. Break down how they should act in an easy to understand, step-by-step manner and give clear, age-appropriate reasons for the desired behavior.

Teachers and caregivers should never assume that a child will pick up lacking executive skills through simple observation. Clearly and calmly teaching the skill by breaking it down into easily understood steps, along with providing appropriate support, is what every adult in their life should do. Remember, children do not have world experience like adults. What they hear, see, and understand in any given situation is vastly different from the viewpoint of an adult.

Incorporate Fun Activities

Learning is best when it's fun. Kids who are already inattentive shouldn't be expected to sit through lectures all day with nothing to break up the monotony. Classroom games have so many benefits, even for kids who don't struggle with the typical schoolroom environment. Some fun ways to get students with various learning styles interested are:

- Charades
- Scavenger hunt
- Math/history/science bingo
- Invent a solution—propose a problem, it doesn't matter how big or small, and allow students to invent creative solutions
- Hangman
- Cut and paste projects
- Building block towers
- Recall games

Personal Support as Parent or Caregiver

It's not uncommon for parents to overestimate how quickly skills will be learned. Remember that these are kids and they have real and valid reasons for acting the way they do. Some parents go to great lengths to set up a certain system that works and then stop following through after one or two successes. Scaffolding should stay in place long-term, even if the methods used for support change over time.

Caregivers should be easily available to answer questions at appropriate times. Many have found success in family work-time at the dinner table. The child sets up their school work area at one end, while a parent sets up their work or household management materials at the other end. This ensures easy access to the parent at a critical time and models the appropriate behavior, showing them that 'homework' doesn't end when school is over.

Above all, parents should be there to offer an understanding and sympathetic ear. It's not the job of parents to be friends, but it is their job to be compassionate when their child is struggling. Since it's often the case that they don't have many friends from their peer group, they may crave methods of connection that are usually common among peers, like learning popular dances.

4

PROVIDING SUPPORT FOR THE CHILD

Providing care for a child with executive function deficiencies is a challenging but rewarding task. It's imperative to be a strong support as they will need more help with mundane tasks than their peers. This will likely remain true in some form or another throughout childhood, and possibly even into early adulthood. Both they and their caregiver need to understand that an executive function disorder or delay isn't a learning disability—although it may accompany such a diagnosis. Many great minds throughout history likely had issues with planning, organization, and/or self-regulation. Albert Einstein is noted to have had quite a messy desk, and many have referred to his office as organized chaos. He finds himself in good company. Mark Zuckerberg, Steve Jobs, and Mark Twain are all known to keep their working spaces quite cluttered.

In many cases, the child will need more support put in place than just an understanding caregiver. Oftentimes, the school needs to be involved to ensure a proper education with the same opportunities afforded to each student. The modern school system has been a difficult place for children who enjoy alternative learning styles. With the introduction of accommodations and allowances in the classroom, children have the opportunity to receive some instruction in a learning style they are comfortable with. By combining classroom changes with the right structure at home, every child has the opportunity to succeed.

AUTONOMY-SUPPORTIVE PARENTING

Children are just like computers; parenting style and behavior modeling are the programs that directly impact the people they will become. By demonstrating how to solve problems and relate to others in a positive way, the child will have the best chance possible to grow up with highly advanced executive functioning skills. Autonomy-supportive parenting seeks to make the child comfortable with themselves and their abilities. This parenting style is the best method to follow to instill greater executive functioning skills in young children. There needs to be a proper mix of autonomy and scaffolding. The balance is something that will take time to determine and will need to change quite often, especially when there is a recent string of successes.

Few people truly consider what parenting style they would like to practice, and even those who do often find that in high-stress situations, what they *want* to happen and what *actually* happens are two completely different things. Being a parent to a well-adjusted child, especially one who is executive delayed, can often be about assessing and correcting one's own behaviors rather than focusing on the child alone.

In the 1960s, four parenting styles were coined by Diana Baumrind, a parenting researcher. She described the authoritarian, permissive, uninvolved, and authoritative types of parenting.

Autonomy-supportive parenting rolls the best qualities of these four types into one. The goal of this style of parenting is to mold autonomous adults who are free from the control of others. This is accomplished through conscious choices which allow for varying degrees of independence in accordance with the environment and the needs of the child.

Implementing the Autonomy-Supportive Parenting Method

Perhaps the most important component of this method is how to engage with the child. While rules and boundaries are important to learn early on, the tone shouldn't be controlling. Everyone is unique. The exact approach should be tailored to the individual's needs, and plenty of space should be provided for contemplation and expression. When a child needs help with the same mundane tasks regularly, it isn't out of the ordinary for the caregiver to act with annoyance or speak with a nagging tone. Although usually done unconsciously, his behavior can compound current problems. When a child learns or improves on a new task, patience is key, as well as plenty of positive reinforcement. In fact, it's not a bad idea to secretly set them up for success from time to time for a boost to their self-esteem. This is especially important for very young kids because sometimes one success can snowball into many others when confidence is lifted.

The key to successfully providing structure and rules in a child's life is to make it the child's choice to exhibit certain desired behaviors. Instead of creating and enforcing a rule that all toys are to be picked up, simply observe and comment on the situation. For example, "The floor is getting quite messy. Let's put some toys away so we don't trip and get hurt." It's quite common for some rules to become second nature when the reason for a certain action is given. The same statements will need to be repeated multiple times; even kids with high executive function need reminders.

Trust is an important factor in autonomy-supportive parenting. When working with children who have low executive functioning abilities, nothing is instant. Some skills and behaviors can take years to fully develop, but it's vital to trust that those tasks will eventually become easier. Make the child aware that you understand it takes time to learn these things. Acknowledging the difficulty they are having makes them feel understood and accomplished for learning something difficult. These types of conversations go a long way towards calming anxiety and setting the stage for a calm learning environment. It's all too easy to become frustrated by a constantly messy bedroom.

Instead of giving harsh chastisement, consider how a conversation about working together to keep the home cleaner will offer more benefits. To a child with low executive function, being told to clean a messy room—even if they are the creators of said mess—is too overwhelming. Dirty clothes go in the basket, books on the shelf, toys in the bin, blankets folded, etc. These kids often can't wrap their heads around how to complete all these different tasks, and they feel that completing the steps would take entirely too long. If the caregiver offers to organize the books while the child puts away the toys, everyone is happy. The room is clean, and it didn't take long. The child trusts that their parent or caregiver is there to help them, and they will eventually understand that it doesn't take too long to tidy a bedroom. You can design your own bedroom checklist, similar to the table below, to help your child remember what they need to do when cleaning their room.

Bedroom checklist: activity	Complete
Make bed	
Put toys in appropriate bin	
Put dirty clothes in hamper	
Take dishes to sink	
Put away clean clothes	
Wipe down dresser and nightstand	

IS YOUR PARENTING AFFECTING YOUR CHILD'S EXECUTIVE FUNCTION?

Parents and caregivers want what is best for their kids, but often the best course of action is found through trial and error. Quite often, executive function delays mimic behaviors caused by other conditions, which makes it hard for even a doctor to quickly identify the problem with confidence. For the majority of these children, providing a mental health diagnosis is not an exact science and relies heavily on observation. Parents need to be meticulous note-keepers in order to provide the doctor with the most information possible, making specific notes of certain sets of behaviors that don't seem to line up with one another.

Don't be shy about speaking up throughout the process of determining what, if any, disorder your child has. Doctors have the education and knowledge, but you know your child. Ensure they understand the major problem behaviors, even if it's not something the doctor noticed, because children are known to act totally differently around their primary caregiver. It's because that person becomes a safe space where they don't have to hold it all together after a long and stressful day. Although it doesn't seem like it at the time, being a safe space for one of these children is quite possibly the most satisfying and rewarding experience in life.

Seemingly trivial issues seen in small children can become big problems in later years. This isn't always the case, but it is beneficial to err on the side of caution by taking notice of difficulties early in life. The child's pediatrician should be kept informed of any concerning behaviors and will be of assistance in determining if and when outside help should be sought.

It's important to teach skills that foster independence from an early age. Simple matters, like tying shoelaces and zipping up a jacket, provide opportunities to practice age-appropriate self-sufficiency in the toddler years. In today's world, everything seems so rushed. It's often necessary for the parents to perform those simple tasks to ensure the family stays on schedule. However, it's very beneficial long-term to teach self-care skills when the atmosphere is relaxed. Doing so will make a big difference a year or so down the road.

A fun and hands-on way of teaching how to tie shoes without ending up late for every event is to punch some holes in a sheet of construction paper. You will need them in two columns, with the holes lined up evenly across. Lace shoelaces through the holes, using a glue gun to hold them in place if necessary. This way, the child can practice this skill as needed.

Parents know their children better than anyone. That knowledge needs to be put to use by ensuring they aren't pushed too hard. Everyone has limits and certain stimuli that set them off. Anything that could cause a meltdown or additional hardship should be removed, at least until skills are at a more age-appropriate level. The measure of success should not be how many unsavory things a person is able to deal with, but the ability to navigate the world in a contented manner.

When giving instructions, if it's known the child cannot remember more than three steps at a time, they shouldn't be set up for failure by being asked to do something they cannot. Doing so will not actually teach them anything and will only serve to decrease their self-confidence and desire to extend themselves in the future. Instead, give three steps of instruction that will be remembered. After that is completed, check in and give directions for the next portion. After a while, it's likely the child will begin putting the steps together on their own. A little patience, understanding, and space go a long way in setting up a receptive mind conducive to learning.

Consistency is always key, especially when working with children experiencing executive functioning delays. Discipline and conse-quences must be the same over time; inconsistent practice only serves to create a situation where a child who already has difficulty learning from past actions has no solid experience behind them. Responsible parents are those who guide their children to conform to society's standards, while allowing them freedom of choice when appropriate and when consequences are clearly understood.

ASSESS YOUR OWN EXECUTIVE STRENGTHS AND WEAKNESSES

Over the years, the National Education Association and the National Parent Teacher Association have published various recommendations for parents regarding how to best set up the home environment and become more involved with their child's education for the best educational and social outcome. One thing that has not been considered in these studies, however, is the level of executive functioning in the parents. Some parents may seem uninvolved or lazy to an outsider, even though they are highly concerned with their child's development.

If you realize that your own executive functioning skills are lacking, it's important to first work on yourself. Adults generally have an easier time introducing positive executive habits into their lives than children do, but it's still not always possible. It might be the case that the parent will need to first get some professional help themselves before attempting to make changes in the life of their child. It may even be possible to have family sessions where both parties can learn these skills together and hold each other accountable.

Previous generations did not have so much information at their fingertips, and there was a bit of a stigma against speaking with a therapist up until very recently. There are a lot of adults that should be in therapy for some reason or another, and there's no shame in that. The world has changed so completely from what it was like in the not-so-distant past. Our lives are unrecognizable from how they were a century ago. There is nothing surprising about needing help to navigate the modern world. A bit of compassion goes a long way, even for ourselves.

MEET YOUR CHILD WHERE THEY ARE AND GO FROM THERE

These children don't choose to be difficult or cause uncomfortable situations, no matter how it may seem. Life is difficult for them, and they understand this from a very early age. If there was any way to change their troubled behavior other than consistency and patience, their issues would have been solved by now. There's often a mismatch between what children are capable of and what is expected of them. This is even more true when dealing with a child experiencing executive dysfunction.

No child will have perfect executive capabilities, even many adults struggle with some of these skills. Executive functioning skills don't become fully developed until the mid to late 20s for neurotypical children, and even later for children with delays. Try to keep school lighthearted and fun. Stress and gloom don't help and will only serve to decrease motivation. At least for a period of time, understand that these children require a different kind of parenting. Parents should aim to keep an air of patience since the child cannot help what they are unable to change. With time, practice, and maturity, results will begin to manifest when the child is ready to step out more fully into the world.

Be sure the child knows there is nothing wrong with needing some extra help in these matters. Needing extra guidance can make some kids feel ashamed, but their differences should always be something to celebrate. Everyone learns these skills at different rates, and they will catch up in due time.

ENFORCE ACCOUNTABILITY

It's true that these kids have special needs that require special understanding, regardless of the presence of a learning disability. However, they can't get into the mindset that anything is allowed because they have different rules. Parents know the personality and abilities of their children and should not let them get away with slacking or causing trouble on purpose. There should be accountability for their actions; maintaining certain expectations shows the parent has faith in them. Before meting out any consequences, understand where the misbehavior is coming from. Problematic behavior stemming from a lack of executive functioning skills should not be punished because a skill deficit is not the same as willful disobedience. Some ways to enforce accountability include:

- not making excuses for bad behavior.
- writing down punishments for certain actions.
- weekly meetings to discuss their behavior and any upcoming changes to their schedule.
- not allowing the blame game.
- consistency, consistency, consistency.

KEEP AN OPEN MIND

Although parents know their child deeply, it's possible behaviors in school or social settings won't be seen at home. If a teacher or another parent comes to them with difficult information about their child, the first reaction of the parent is often disbelief. It's important not to jump to conclusions, but new information about troubling behaviors should be investigated. On the other hand, teachers need to reciprocate in kind. Parents aren't necessarily lying if a problematic behavior in school has never been seen at home.

Frequently, children who lack certain skills will go out of their way to avoid performing those tasks with which they struggle. Sometimes this can come off as sneaky or deceitful, so absorb the entire context if there has been questionable behavior.

POSITIVITY

Words hurt, no matter what anyone says. Parents really have to be the gatekeeper at times by not allowing those with negative or hurtful things to say about their child to have the opportunity to do so. Kids with executive dysfunction are not lazy, ignorant, or disruptive. They need compassion, understanding, and guidance. When something goes wrong, the parents always need to stay calm. Impulsivity and overreactions are common in executive delayed kids, so yelling doesn't offer any long-term benefits. Calmly rooting out the cause of problematic behavior most certainly will lead to its extinction. A cool head will go a long way when teaching executive functioning skills.

5

SELF-CONTROL AND REGULATION

Controlling impulses, emotions, and behaviors to achieve goals is a key trait of humanity. Our prefrontal cortex is larger than in other mammals, and it's the area of our brain responsible for self-control. It's thought that self-control isn't a stable trait like intelligence, but rather a fluctuating resource akin to physical energy. Throughout the day, self-control waxes and wanes. As such, the uniqueness of this schedule needs to be considered when you set up your own schedule.

Self-control is a complex skill that develops over time and means different things at different stages of life. In the early toddler years, it looks like waiting in line, taking turns, and sitting still for short periods of time. As they grow, they will be expected to temper their responses to unpleasant news and practice delayed gratification in order to complete tasks.

There are three areas of self-control: movement control, impulse control, and emotional control. A well-adjusted individual is able to stay in control of themselves in all three aspects.

- **Movement Control**: Excessive hyperactivity that continues past the toddler years could point to a problem with self-control. It's important for everyone to learn that there is a time and place to be still. However, one must keep the physical needs of the child in mind. A hyperactive child will never be able to behave properly in school if there is not ample opportunity for movement.
- **Impulse Control**: The ability to stop and think before acting. Kids are prone to impulsivity, even into early adulthood. Such behavior should decrease in frequency and intensity as they grow. Although it is a common issue in children, excessive impulsivity is a primary component of many mental health issues. Those with poor impulse control are prone to gambling, stealing, and generally aggressive behavior. Negative behaviors become normalized and habitual over time, generally with increasing intensity. It's important for parents to ensure their kids are learning to control their actions in age-appropriate ways.
- **Emotional Control**: It's important for kids to keep going even when plans change or something upsetting happens. Focus should shift away from the immediate unpleasantness and onto a future goal. It's a good idea to ensure children have the language and ability to communicate their emotions as early as possible. Impulsive children often don't have the self-awareness to label emotions and properly explain what they are feeling. A child who is unable to recognize or articulate that they are angry is more likely to hit.

PROBLEMS FROM A LACK OF SELF-CONTROL

This is a critical skill that begins to develop early in life. It's important for parents to ensure their child is able to control themselves in appropriate ways throughout their youth, as other executive functioning skills depend greatly on the continued development of self-control. Issues with self-control call for immediate action as the outcome for adults lacking this skill is not good. Health problems like obesity and drug dependency are common. They're also more likely to be incarcerated and less likely to be wealthy.

Tantrums are common in kids with low levels of self-control. These episodes are rather intense and continue later into childhood than would be expected, and their overactivity manifests in various ways. Talking can seem non-stop, and interrupting peers and blurting out answers in class can strain relationships at school. They may cut in line without thinking or grab things without asking the owner first. Sensitivity to criticism is another hallmark quality of low self-control and will often cause the child to completely give up on a task. They may cry or become excessively upset at light teasing.

Children lacking this skill really do suffer, and they truly would love an opportunity to change. By the time they enter early elementary school, they are usually very much aware of the differences between them and their peers, as well as the difficulties their behavior brings.

BUILDING SELF-CONTROL

Meeting the child at the level they are currently at is vital in making a difference in building their level of self-control. A child who is unable to take turns will not be able to sit quietly for a class lecture, but it's unfair to expect complex behaviors before mastering the previous steps. Children are impatient by nature, so a child who lacks self-control shouldn't be expected to practice patience for extended periods. Frequent play breaks are often necessary for toddlers and early elementary kids.

Also, be very clear about what to expect and what is expected of them in a particular situation. Many children react poorly to surprises or unexpected difficulties, so be honest if they have to participate in an activity that is boring or time-consuming. Let them know what they have to look forward to after the event. Perhaps after patiently running errands, there's a trip to the playground planned.

The benefits of self-control can never be overstated. Everything worth having in life is going to take some work, and the sooner the child understands that, the better it will be for them. A common test given to young elementary-aged kids is the marshmallow test. It's a good way to test the limits of your child's sense of self-control and delayed gratification. In this experiment, a marshmallow is placed in front of the child. They are then given two choices:

1. Eat the one marshmallow now; or
2. Don't touch the marshmallow, and in five minutes, receive another one.

During those five minutes, all adults will leave the room, and the child will be alone with the marshmallow and a video camera. Some kids are able to wait at least somewhat patiently, thereby doubling the size of their sweet treat. Some kids have not mastered the notion of delayed gratification and would rather have a smaller snack so long as they can have it now, or perhaps they very much wish to have the ability to wait but are unable to do so. This simple and fun exercise can show parents early on that their child needs some extra support in developing self-control.

As always, any opportunity for positive reinforcement should be seized. Offer lots of praise when they behave correctly and practice self-control. Kids feel great about themselves when they overcome an obstacle.

Rules

Although it may seem like these kids fight rules at every turn, they actually crave clear expectations and structure. At the same time, they do not like to feel constricted. It's not a good idea to give a plethora of rules to anyone, not even the most misbehaved of children. Structure is required, but it doesn't have to feel overwhelming. Generally, rules can be condensed into a few basic understandings that can be applied everywhere and to everyone. Yes, even Mommy, Daddy, Granny, and Gramps follow these same rules. It's a good idea to formulate the wording of the rules in a way that makes it clear that they apply to the entire household. Some examples of clear and wide-ranging rules are:

- Treat everyone—including yourself—and their things with respect.
- Don't be wasteful.
- Follow the schedule whenever possible.

Generally, if these three rules are followed, there will be no misbehaving unless there are special instructions for a specific purpose. Sometimes, a certain activity has different rules or expectations. Be sure they are prepared for whatever is happening around them.

· · ·

Phrasing

Try and have the child repeat certain phrases, even if they're having trouble with the activity. By saying, "I'll wait my turn, it's okay," when it's clearly NOT okay can help change their mindset and avoid a tantrum. Even if the child doesn't want to repeat it, the parents should repeat the phrase calmly.

Parents and teachers should talk to children clearly and simply. Many children who struggle with self-control have ADHD or autism. They may take words and phrases literally, so be sure not to use phrases that have an alternate meaning. For example, if a child asks their mother for a sandwich and she responds, "Just a second," that could cause a meltdown fairly quickly. When the mother says she will make the sandwich in a second, but it takes her two minutes to start, the child feels frustrated and ignored.

Routine

Routines are important for children, and a schedule with some thought behind it will have a big impact. Many teachers find it helpful to plan for story time right before recess. This way, the active kids have a reward for sitting still before playtime, having an opportunity to practice and succeed in developing self-control.

Predictability is key. What the day looks like should be spelled out from the beginning. Any deviation from the plan should be explained, as well as what will now be expected of them. Timely reminders are a good idea so expectations do not get lost in time or excitement.

Kids learn by repetitive behavior. If all of their days looked different, they would be unable to predict the order of things or successfully set up their own daily schedule. Even if daily activities change often, it's good practice to wake up, eat, bathe, and sleep at consistent times.

Consequences

Natural consequences are an excellent teacher, and the job is done with little to no parental involvement. Nature, society, or other people often negatively respond to certain behaviors. By allowing nature to mete out the correction without interference, the lesson is quickly learned, with the real-life application readily understood.

There are many different ways to allow natural consequences to be a teacher; parents and caregivers should only interfere if safety is a concern. The ways in which this method is appropriate will change over time. Perhaps the consequence of refusing to wear mittens should be the resulting cold hands. Or if a healthy and normally enjoyed meal is refused, a hungry belly at night is a wonderful way to learn the importance of meals. When working with a very young child, freezing hands and hungry bellies should be avoided, but there's nothing wrong with leaving toys out in the rain to rust if they don't want to help bring them inside.

At times, the caregiver must interfere to ensure the child understands when a behavior is inappropriate. For example, a child who shoplifts may or may not get caught. If they do not get into trouble with the police, the only consequence would be free stuff. In this case, the parent should make the child return the items with an apology and ground them from anything except school. For recurring negative actions, caregivers should remind them what the punishment will be.

Emotional Coaching

Just because kids lack world experience doesn't mean they don't have big feelings. Be sure to talk to them about their emotions and moods. It's helpful to talk these things out while determining a solution. Show empathy for them and their feelings. By trying to see a situation from their perspective, they feel respected and understood.

Although some feelings may be misdirected, it's important not to punish the child for showing negative emotions. It's best to avoid emotional coaching when they're in a poor mood. Give them understanding and space, then discuss what behaviors were inappropriate while explaining and modeling the desired behavior.

Constant sources of stress need to be addressed. Many adults feel like schoolchildren have no responsibilities and, therefore, no reason to feel stressed. This couldn't be further from the truth and it shows a lack of respect for real people with real problems that children are. School is demanding, and the real world is even more so. Stress can be a natural by-product of such an environment. Even so, chronic stress can lead to all types of health problems— both physical and psychological. Stomach troubles, sleep disturbances, and changes in appetite often manifest, as well as brain chemistry issues like depression, anxiety, and the social complications of being overly emotional. Root out the causes of major sources of stress and do whatever is needed to eliminate them. Even as adults, we often have the right to cut out sources of stress from our lives.

Alternatives

It can be hard for these kids, always being told what not to do. Although they likely don't have more rules than others in their peer group, it seems that way because the constant lack of control means being told 'No' so often. It's helpful to offer alternatives where applicable.

Just like adults, kids can get bored with the same schedule, same options, and no choice or excitement. For example, Kerry may have a plan in place to work on her study skills by making detailed guides before a test. After practicing this system for a while, she complains that her hands cramp from all the writing. It makes the whole process unsavory. An acceptable alternative would be to allow Kerry to make photocopies of the class material and highlight the information she needs to spend time studying, while making extra notes in the margins as needed. This ensures the task of preparing for the test is accomplished, but it's done in a way that is palatable to Kerry.

Sometimes, an alternative can be given without the child's knowledge. This usually only works with young children and isn't advisable with older teens, who may feel lied to when sneaky methods are employed. If a child cries every night for ice cream, regardless of whether they have already had a sweet that day, there's an alternative. Instead of saying no, why not replace the ice cream with a healthier choice? All that's needed are some popsicle molds and a blender. It's easy to make popsicles out of whole, fresh fruit. For a creamier texture, add milk or yogurt for a bit of extra protein.

Prevention

Nobody knows the child like their parents. Parents are in a unique position to reduce possible triggers in the home environment. A child who continually draws on the walls, even when given plenty of paper for artwork, should have the crayons removed for a period of time. Removal of the object shouldn't be thought of as a punishment, but rather as a way to prevent an action that will involve a punishment. Explain this to the child while staying calm and non-confrontational. It's important to meet the child where they are and remove temptations when it's known their self-control is not up to par.

Games

Games are a great way to teach kids about listening and self control. It gets them into a receptive state of mind and makes them feel excited to listen to directions. Simon Says is great fun for younger children. The parent or teacher gives a simple command, such as, "Stand on one leg," or "Sit down." The child only follows directions that are preceded by the words, "Simon says."

When there is excess physical energy, a superb choice is, "red light, green light." When the parent says, "Green light," it's time to run. Their child keeps running until they hear, "Red light!" when they come to a quick stop. Change it up and keep it interesting by throwing a, "Yellow light!" out every once in a while. This gets young children into a state of mind receptive to the idea of learning more advanced executive functioning skills and gives practice with basic listening, working memory, and following directions. They get used to the idea that listening closely to those who care for and teach them is fun. For older kids, playing chess or learning a musical instrument is a great way to learn self-control and strategy.

Take this concept a step further and determine what aspects of game nights are the most pleasing to the child. Do they like the colors or songs? What about rhyming or dancing? Try to incorporate the most enjoyable aspects of games into learning activities. Learn some fun math songs—YouTube is a great resource when used the right way—and make up a silly dance together. I bet the concept will be easily remembered now.

. . .

Calming Corner

Creating a calming corner can be done easily and cheaply. Massive results have been seen from having an area specifically meant to calm down. Many teachers are devoting a corner of their classroom to this purpose, whether or not they have students who have IEPs requiring such a space. Many parents find it helpful to have a similar space at home as well. There's no need for this to be a costly endeavor, although there are a plethora of posters and decorations that can be purchased online. A decorated poster board, along with some calming photos taken from magazines, gets the job done. A bean bag makes a nice spot to rest while reading calming quotes surrounded by light and airy colors. A calming corner serves to create an immediate atmosphere that serves to de-escalate an excited child, often stopping problems before they happen.

Learning to calm down is an important skill. Focus helps a person stay alert, practice self-control, and improve their working memory. However, children cannot learn to focus unless they learn how to calm down when they're over-excited.

6

GET FOCUSED

Focus is an interesting concept when it comes to executive functioning because all of these kids are able to focus on certain topics. The problem arises because there is an inability to choose *what* to focus on. This is an important skill in today's fast-paced world. There's an overabundance of sights, sounds, and ideas that threaten to derail carefully laid plans. Children have to learn from a young age that just because something is vying for their attention doesn't make it important.

Building on self-control, focus also requires a good working memory to remember rules and steps. There are four components that determine the ability of a child to concentrate on a task.

- **Focus**: Being alert, attentive, and orienting. Orienting means the ability to focus on specific tasks relating to one goal.
- **Cognitive flexibility**: The ability to adjust to environmental changes and understand various perspectives.

- **Working memory**: A mental scratch pad. Information in working memory can be manipulated, changed, or updated. Working memory is helpful for comparing and contrasting similar situations that have previously occurred.
- **Inhibitory control**: Self-control of emotions, actions, thoughts, and behaviors so that specific tasks may be performed.

HOW TO HELP YOUR CHILD FOCUS

Because there are four components to focus on—one of them being self-control—children should be given ample opportunity to learn and observe a state of calm. An excited mind is likely to remain unfocused. Being a good example of patience and planning from the early years will give the child the best possible start.

There are many tips and tricks available to build focus, and all children benefit from the extra attention in this area, whether or not it's specifically needed. The world is becoming very loud and fast, full of information of all types. Slowing down enough to accurately take in and filter information is a skill that will go a long way.

Give Attention to Get Attention

It's a hard, if not impossible, task to instill the value of focus in a child without first focusing on them. When giving instructions, be close to them. Don't shout instructions from across the room. Speak quietly, and calmly, and make eye contact. Parents and instructors should be an example.

Let your child see you waiting and being patient. Yes, it seems to take an eternity for them to put on their shoes, but it will be accomplished. Wait patiently without rushing. While it's true that most adults depend on their phones for most aspects of life, many use them to distract themselves from waiting. This is the wrong signal to send to a child and often seems unfair. Kids, by nature, have less patience than adults and are often held to a higher standard.

Get into the habit of reading to your child on a regular basis. This should happen throughout childhood. The subject of the story isn't important, but the act of listening to the parents is an important behavior that's encouraged by frequent reading.

Explore Different Ways of Learning

Kids can be goofy. It's a good idea to make lessons fun so they can be their silly selves. During story time, use different voices, intonations, and sound effects that make the story more engaging and memorable. Early elementary-aged children are still building their vocabulary. When the story is told in an emotive voice, they are better able to understand new words.

Hands-on and messy lesson plans are a great idea for these kids for so many reasons. All people are hard-wired to pay attention to abnormal occurrences. It's easy to see why this has such great appeal. Lesson plans that include multiple senses are more attention-grabbing in comparison to listening to a lecture.

Remember, just because most students seem to perform well when education takes place, doesn't mean they won't benefit from having a chance to physically move, especially before a task that requires being quiet and still. This is beneficial for all students. Remember that these skills exist on a spectrum. Not all students who have issues with focus need as much help; those who fall in the middle of the spectrum often get left behind.

Make It Exciting

Everyone has something that gets them excited, so find out what it is your child is happy to focus on and put it at the forefront of their educational experience. A lack of focus often comes from not engaging with the material. Of course, all subjects are important and deserving of focus, but until this skill is learned, there is not much information that will be absorbed. As a student is preparing for their science fair, they should really work hard to ensure the subject matter is of great interest to them. Any opportunity that creates a desire to know should be seized. Also, any opportunity to do work of the students' choosing, like a book report, should be taken advantage of since personalized education can make such a difference in their lives.

There is no shortage of fun games that help focus the attention of children of all ages. I-spy, red light/green light, Simon says, and musical chairs are easy enough for the youngest kids to learn, and fun enough to remain exciting over many years. Older kids and teens may enjoy guessing games like 20 questions, Pictionary, or charades. Many people don't realize how beneficial such entertainment can be, as it isn't necessarily educational. The importance of a relaxed and joyful mind in learning cannot be overstated, and these games all incorporate listening and gathering information from outside sources.

Playing pretend is an excellent way to keep a child's mind focused. It takes a lot of concentration to stay in character, plus, working memory is challenged by manipulating what is known about how a new character would behave. Role-playing games don't stop as the child gets older; they just become a bit more grown-up in nature. Mock-trials are a great way to get kids to understand the judicial system by playing out an actual role. The debate team may have them argue the opposing side in order to gain a big-picture understanding. Later on, mock interviews will be helpful in easing the transition into adulthood.

Dedicated Workspace

A lack of organization and planning is sure to lead to a lack of focus. By keeping a dedicated workspace—filled with all the necessary tools—the student will be set up for success. It's a good idea to encourage—and help, if needed—tidying up the space after work is completed. This way, when the child is ready to work, there are no additional tasks of collecting supplies. It's hard enough to get a child lacking focus to sit down and work; this helps the process go as smoothly and easily as possible.

The atmosphere needs to remain calm. An over-excited mind has trouble remembering new information. Pay attention to the things that are able to bring the child down from an excited state and make frequent use of such techniques. Controlling their bodies, emotions, and actions is a new skill as the toddler and early elementary years are left behind. Any approach that makes this easier and doesn't interfere with their education should be employed.

Giving Direction

Don't go overboard when giving instructions. Explicitly explaining one or two steps at a time before moving forward eases anxiety about remembering directions. More focus will be on the specific task-at-hand, rather than struggling to remember. This helps students jump right into the assignment without delay. When tasks are delayed, it becomes harder to get started.

Directions should be given in very clear, unambiguous language. "First/then" or "if/then" statements describe the sequence in an easy-to-understand way. For example, "If you get cleaned up, then we can go to the movies" states what has to be accomplished before a reward can be given. "First go to the toilet, then get in the shower," gives the correct order, so there is no confusion regarding how to start.

Direct Their Focus

Reprimanding a student for not focusing is not going to teach the skill, and it can often cause embarrassment when done in front of their peers. By the time they are in school, children who lack focus know this is a shortcoming, although they may not always realize it when they begin to lose focus. There are ways to get them back on track without drawing attention to them in a negative way. Ask a question that they know the answer to or pat them on the shoulder in passing. Doing something like this has the effect of bringing them back to earth before they get too far behind on their work. Also, give all students an opportunity to ask questions at this point. This allows the student struggling with focus to catch something they might have missed without drawing attention. A teacher may also come up with a secret word that brings attention to the lack of focus. Working together will always see better results than trying to force behavior without the child's understanding. Get together and brainstorm ways to bring focus back.

Screen Time

It's becoming apparent how damaging constant screen time can be for all kids, even teenagers. Young children should have no more than 30 minutes daily, and many experts advise that it's best to eliminate it all together. Sometimes, life gets hectic and they may end up using electronic devices far more than what is healthy. In these cases, a screen removal might be necessary. It will take a few weeks for the child's neurological system to reset—during this time, all electronics should be removed.

As the child ages; however, computers, tablets, and electronic devices will become a mainstay in their life. It's so important to model and enforce proper usage. During this stage, electronic usage should be closely monitored to ensure it is being used for mostly educational purposes.

Helpful Tools

Many useful gadgets exist that are helpful in directing focus. Since many children who need a bit of help focusing have ADHD or a sensory processing disorder (SPD), it is logical to dull some of their overactive senses when their focus should be directed inward. Earplugs and noise-canceling headphones are great for this purpose, and they are not distracting or disruptive in a classroom setting. By physically blocking things that may be distracting, privacy dividers can help direct focus to the task at hand. Fidget toys are great for children with high excitability. Fidget spinners became all the rage a few years ago, although many teachers disliked them as they could be a bit distracting to other students. A stress ball is a good option to keep their hands busy without disrupting other students.

The use of a timer can make a world of difference, both in the classroom and at home. It's easier to focus when it's understood ahead of time how long that focus must be held. The length of time can and should gradually increase as long as there remains ample opportunity for movement, snacks, and restroom breaks. There are no rewards in life for being uncomfortable, and no reason for a child to try and stay focused when they are hungry.

BOOSTING WORKING MEMORY AND PROCESSING SPEED

A lack of focus can cause problems utilizing working memory. This is a short-term function of the brain and works somewhat like a post-it note. It's where information is stored for a particular task-at-hand. Think of a very advanced math student. When the teacher is explaining a problem, they see the numbers in their mind, and are able to manipulate and change them along with the teacher. It may also be true that ten minutes later, the student will have no recollection of the exact numbers in the problem, but that's beside the point. Working memory is information relevant to the task at hand. If there is no benefit to remembering exact information, it is best to throw that post-it away and start fresh. Some information used in this way needs to be stored in long-term memory. It's a way of organizing and understanding details before filing them away for later use.

It's important to note that the human brain has a finite ability to store information, even for those with advanced scholarly abilities. This is vital for educators and parents alike to understand as the world moves into a future where comparatively massive amounts of data are needed to perform daily tasks. Rote memorization, which still holds importance for standardized testing and building a base of knowledge in the early years, is becoming a thing of the past in adult endeavors. Learning to research and quickly filter data is an important skill to bring into a new era of information.

Problems with working memory are most easily observed as difficulty remembering directions. The order in which tasks are to be accomplished may get jumbled or left out entirely. There may be problems performing mental math, especially with equations involving more than one step. Also, when the information is recalled at a later time, it may not make much sense. Those who have trouble with working memory often experience a snowball effect of time management being affected. The good news is, there are plenty of ways to increase working memory and brain processing speed; a few tips and tricks can make all the difference.

Write It Down

Physically recording information is the best way to increase memory. It's just like plugging an external hard drive into a computer. Albert Einstein, whose theories and equations were based on the speed of light, did not actually memorize what that exact speed was. He said, "[I do not] carry such information in my mind since it is readily available in books… The value of a college education is not the learning of many facts, but the training of the mind to think" (Fake, 2014).

Have the child keep a notebook handy to write down information about things they are currently working on. They can keep track of the daily schedule, homework assignments, sports practices, and ideas for new projects. Make it exciting and they will naturally start to remember many of the notes they jot down and refer to over time.

Multitasking

Multitasking should be introduced to young children as a way of breaking up large tasks into easily digestible components. It's not a good idea to encourage early elementary age kids to work on many activities at once. The finished product is often sloppy—if it's even finished—while the child feels anxious about the result. As the child grows up, multitasking will become necessary in some way or another. It's then helpful to teach prioritization and detailed scheduling. There are three primary methods one may use when multitasking: Classic multitasking, rapid task switching, and interrupted task switching.

Classic multitasking happens when we intentionally try to do multiple things at the same time. Some examples of this type would be texting while driving, or helping kids with homework while cooking dinner. The results are rarely good, so it's best to discourage this behavior with young ones.

Rapid task switching is similar, in that multitasking is intentional but the activities are not done simultaneously. Having a web browser open and switching between multiple tabs constantly is an example of this and is classic ADHD behavior.

Interrupted task switching is multitasking that is more or less forced. An example of this would be working on a school project while getting a phone call that has to be taken right away.

Multitasking is not always a bad thing. Riding a stationary bike while chatting with a friend won't cause any excess stress, and it's an important skill to learn. A good rule of thumb is to ensure only **one** cognitive activity is done at a time, whenever possible. Turning off notifications or setting a timer before switching to a different task are things that can help improve both concentration and results.

Most people believe they are better at multitasking than they actually are. A lot of time can be wasted switching back and forth between tasks because the start-up time needed to begin over and over again is more than it seems and adds up quickly. It's a far better use of time to practice chunking. This is when the day is broken up into many chunks of time that are each used to focus on one specific task.

Developing Habits and Routines

Routines are so important, especially in children with executive function delays, because eventually the routine will become a habit. This is a huge step in boosting mental capacity; working memory will not be needed for day-to-day tasks, freeing space for other endeavors. It's helpful to have a simple checklist for routines that we, as adults, think are so easy. Besides laying out the steps one-by-one, it's a positive experience for some children to check off activities as they are completed. It gives a feeling of accomplishment and satisfaction that should be felt after a complex task is completed.

Morning routine checklist	Complete
Shower	
Get dressed	
Eat breakfast	
Brush teeth	
Gather school supplies	
Walk to the bus stop	

Consistency is key. Find a routine that works and stick with it. Patience on the part of the parent is needed here, as it takes time for a routine to become a habit. All too often, parents give up on a routine when it doesn't seem to be working, but over time it will become second nature. Offer plenty of reminders and give lots of praise when children follow the schedule in an easygoing way.

FLEXIBLE THINKING

Stubbornness and rigid thinking lead to negative results in everyone, but especially in children. This is the time that they should be taking in as much information as possible, and observing things from many angles and perspectives. It's a tough task to educate a stubborn child. Some signs of rigid thinking in children are:

- Not accepting other points of view.
- Making the same argument multiple times.
- Trouble switching from task-to-task.
- Difficulty with new schedules.
- Anxiety over changes in plans.
- Frustration when things go wrong.
- Trouble understanding jokes.
- Making the same mistakes .

Plans should be made to encourage flexible thinking as solutions are more readily available to kids who can think outside the box. Incentify flexible thinking by:

- **Providing visual or verbal cues before or during an activity**: When all of the children run to the petting zoo instead of towards the cake and ice cream, like Dylan expected, tell him that cake can come later, it's OK to do things in a different order. This cues Dylan to join his friends in the activity that they most want to take part in first, because not everything has to happen in a stringent order.
- **Playing strategy and logic games**: Kids love playing games and are forever wanting their parents' attention during the early, formative years. Ensure the games played serve educational, as well as entertainment, purposes. Children's games like checkers and tic-tac-toe are great choices for young elementary-age children, while games

like chess and 20 questions will be more desirable for older kids.

- **Creating new rules for games**: Who says games have to be played the way the instructions say? Practice coming up with your own rules and see who can make the most interesting game. This works exceptionally well for well-loved games that may have lost a few pieces over the years.
- **Wordplay**: Words can have multiple meanings. Introduce the idea of puns to young kids and the whole family will be sure to have fun making their own inside jokes throughout the years.
- **Playing pretend**: All kids love role-play, and this game doesn't have to stop for older kids, just make it more grown-up. Have your high school kids write a screenplay for any subject matter that is important at the time. Record the play on video and use editing apps to create a one-of-a-kind project.
- **Finding multiple uses for objects**: How many ways can this spatula be used? Of course it's made for cooking eggs, but could it also be useful for mixing that pitcher of lemonade?

Perhaps the most fun executive skill to teach and learn, flexible thinking ideals are found in the most interesting games and offer feelings of control—something all kids crave. Fannee Doolee is a goofy game that will have young spellers on their toes and thinking flexibly. Fannee really likes double letters, so she prefers eggs to egos. She also drinks coffee but doesn't like tea quite as much. She loves to play in the grass and stays away from dirt. Have a laugh while taking turns coming up with pairs of words that Fannee either likes or dislikes.

Math games can be just as much fun. It's helpful for students when important skills are taught in the context of different subjects. Gather up some small items that are likely scattered throughout the house or classroom. Crayons, beads, or buttons work great. Ask, "How many ways can I make the number seven?" and have the child add different amounts of different items that all equal seven. Take turns picking numbers and coming up with solutions.

Another interesting and challenging game is called "Yes, and…" It is a wonderfully simple way to really bring about creative thinking and story-telling. One person makes a statement, such as, "It is snowing today." The other player responds, "Yes, and I left my gloves at home." The next player adds yet another statement, saying something like, "Yes, and I really wanted to build a snow-man." Kids love to discover what kind of creative story they can invent with the collaboration of others.

While it's a huge benefit in academic and social settings, teaching a child how to practice flexible thinking is one of the best things that can be done to benefit them in the future. Coming up with innovative solutions to problems is the best way to get ahead and achieve your dreams. Just because flexible thinking is a more creative skill doesn't mean that it doesn't have real, practical applications that can achieve amazing results. In fact, flexible thinking combined with working memory and focus feeds directly into time management skills.

7

TIME MANAGEMENT

Mentally, there is a lot involved in time management. This skill is far more complex than simple scheduling. The most important aspect of time management is having an accurate understanding of time and how activities flow into one another. This knowledge is used to make decisions regarding the best way to complete responsibilities and meet deadlines. Effective time management will lead to increased productivity and efficiency.

Many tools exist that help manage schedules across the whole range of technological capabilities. Don't be shy about the idea of technology assisting children in understanding this skill. Not many can name an adult that doesn't use some sort of electronic device for this reason.

An environment conducive to work is of the utmost importance. The area should be calm and free of clutter, with anything that will be needed within easy reach. Some children, especially those with ADHD, work better with a bit of background noise. The extra bit of stimulation seems to help them remain still enough to work. This can be done with low, relaxing music in the background at home or with headphones in the classroom, provided the music is not loud enough to become disruptive to others. In areas such as the classroom, parents and teachers may need to determine if the child is eligible for an Individual Education Plan (IEP) or a 504 plan to ensure that the child is receiving the correct accommodations, if they have not already done so.

Motivation is one of the greatest determining factors of one's time management abilities. One of the worst things to say to a kid is; *because I said so.* They should know *why* the things they have to do are important. Goals are important for all ages, and there's a purpose for all the tasks that must be accomplished. One of the best pieces of advice when it comes to time management is to cut out distractions. Without an understanding of the reason or end goal, they may consider important tasks to be unimportant.

Without a solid awareness of how time flows, it is impossible to estimate how long different activities will take. It's no surprise that children with time management issues experience difficulty with prioritizing different items on their schedule and effectively pacing themselves. This is likely the easiest skill to get children excited about. Who doesn't like being in charge of how they spend their time? Parents and educators need to be explicit when they teach time management techniques and not try to 'hide' what they are really teaching. The amount of control over day-to-day life cannot be stressed enough.

SIGNS OF TIME MANAGEMENT ISSUES

All of childhood, even the teenage years, is filled with learning new things and thinking in far more complex ways. All children, no matter how excellent their executive functioning skills are, will seem to struggle with managing their time on occasion. What's important is to note how long it takes to master a skill so it can be accomplished relatively quickly and independently. More often than not, those kids who learn differently need a bit of extra assistance managing their day-to-day life.

A third grader completing a book report will need lots of help along the way to ensure this complex assignment is finished correctly. A parent should assist in choosing the book, scheduling enough time to read every day, discussing the book, and formatting the report. Some children may catch on quickly and only need help with the first report, while others require varying degrees of parental involvement for a period of time. Both scenarios are normal; however, a fifth or sixth grader should be able to complete the assignment without help and relatively quickly. Some other signs of time management issues are:

- Takes excessive time completing tasks.
- Unable to move forward when getting stuck on one part of the assignment.
- Neglecting tasks due tomorrow to work on something due next week.
- Unable to complete tasks even though they are working consistently.
- Rushing.
- Impatience.
- Difficulty with morning routine.
- Poor performance on timed tests.

It's difficult to determine issues with time management skills in young children as they are not able to accomplish many complex tasks with multiple steps alone. However, extreme impatience can be an early sign that points to a disconnect in the understanding of the passage of time and sequences of events. A toddler who throws a tantrum because he wants to go to the playground now—not in an hour—may not realize that the hour is filled with tasks needing completion before leaving home. There's lots to do in preparation for a trip, and this is the perfect time to introduce the idea of planning. Filling up water bottles, packing a snack, loading and turning on the dishwasher, and feeding the dog need to be finished before an afternoon of fun. Explain what needs to be done and that it will be a busy hour of preparation to leave. Suggest the child help, and maybe it will be possible to complete the chores a bit early.

Most children exhibiting any executive functioning delays likely have issues with time management as well. Low working memory makes it difficult to remember different pieces of information that are important to the task-at-hand. A lack of focus leads to being sidetracked often, and rigid thinking makes it difficult to understand that different tasks take different amounts of time. Add in hyperactivity and complex tasks seem like a recipe for disaster. However, teaching time management skills can be accomplished with some planning and patience from all parties involved.

HOW TO TEACH TIME MANAGEMENT SKILLS

Time management skills require practice. When there's an accurate understanding of time, the child has the ability to estimate how long tasks will take and schedule accordingly. This can only be accomplished through continual awareness of time while working.

Teaching this skill requires lots of scheduling, and it's always important for the child to be involved in creating that schedule. To do that, they must first be aware of the passage of time as they go through the day. A stopwatch is an easy and fun way for them to learn about time management. Have them time themselves getting ready in the morning, traveling to school, eating lunch, doing homework, etc. Keep this learning opportunity stress-free by scheduling much needed breaks throughout the day. A child who consistently has trouble completing tasks can easily become overwhelmed during this process. Brain breaks should consist of enjoyable activities, and plenty of tasks that the child is able to perform well should be included in the daily schedule. Ensure that kids are not overscheduled. It is important to process the events of the day and learn how to utilize downtime. Use the daily schedule example below to help your child create a plan that details how they would spend their day.

Daily Schedule Example

Time	Activity
6:00-6:30	wake up/shower
6:30-7:00	eat breakfast
7:00-7:30	brush teeth/gather supplies/leave for bus stop
7:30-2:30	school
2:45-3:30	choir practice
4:00-4:15	arrive home/eat snack
4:15-6:00	homework—5 minute brain break every 25 minutes
6:00-6:30	TV/tablet time
6:30-7:30	dinner/family time
7:30-8:30	bath/brush teeth/prepare clothes and supplies for the morning
8:30-9:00	wind-down/story time
9:00	bedtime

Keep time estimates in mind when creating the schedule and record the approximate time allocation. Update the schedule daily, weekly, and monthly. It should be displayed in the same location every day. Sometimes a more detailed morning schedule may be needed, especially with younger children. See the table in Chapter 6 for an example of a more detailed morning schedule.

Older kids will start to have more long-term projects as they advance in school. It's helpful to create mini-deadlines along the way. This technique is helpful for keeping the correct pace. Be sure to add a bit of organization time to the schedule. It doesn't have to be much; 10 minutes in the morning and evening should be sufficient to keep an orderly workspace and update the calendar.

Discuss prioritization and help determine what assignments are the most important. First, list all homework assignments, then rank them in order of importance. The most time consuming assignments, or those with the closest due dates, need to be accomplished first. Let the child help determine the correct order. The assignment with the closest due date may be finished on Sunday evening rather than Saturday morning because the child has an easier time concentrating when the excitement of the hockey tournament has passed. Identify some easily attainable goals that can be broken down into small pieces.

It can be helpful to introduce the SMART method of goal setting, which takes into account everything that goes into a specific goal. The goal must be specific, measurable, attainable, relevant, and time-oriented. The best type of goal to use with the SMART method is one that is rather unique. It's advisable to avoid vague behaviors when using this chart. The activity should be able to be objectively measured. Consider whether work is completed on schedule, the quality of work, and the amount of effort required by the child. It is so important to build self-esteem in children, so ensure the task is something within their ability to complete. An activity that is relevant is one that can be easily fit into the schedule of the child and aligns with their interests and goals. The SMART method is best when employed for short-term projects. Larger assignments can benefit from this method as well, but it may be best if long-term projects are broken up into smaller, more easily digestible pieces. Below is an example of a worksheet that Toby might complete when he sets a goal of entering a short story contest.

Specific	**M**easurable	**A**ttainable	**R**elevant	**T**ime-Orientated
Enter the short-story contest. Admissions due by November 13th.	Set aside half an hour on Tuesdays and Thursdays to work on the submission. Aim to write 500 words per day.	Resources needed: computer, notebook, pens, books/stories for inspiration, grammar book/notes, and a quiet working space.	There is ample time to work on the project. Toby's writing skills have improved, and he wants to challenge himself.	The finished story is due in two months. There is plenty of time to complete the project if the schedule is followed.

Teach the importance of moving on when stuck on a portion of the assignment. It's OK to come back to a confusing portion at a later time. If they are still stuck, they can reread the instructions, or ask a parent or teacher for guidance if it's unclear how to move forward. Provide reminders when time is almost over. Giving both a five and ten-minute warning is a good idea because it can be stressful to hear the warning with just a short time left to work.

Talk frequently about distractions and how to avoid them when necessary. There's nothing wrong with watching a favorite show in the evening, but past experience says that half an hour may turn into an hour and a half. It's best to complete the math assignment first, so there's nothing to worry about later. Use clocks and timers to show how much time can be wasted on the couch, it always ends up being much more than anyone imagines. Television is not the only "time-eater" out there, and many such activities aren't always bad. An artist can spend all day drawing, and while it's important to capitalize on strengths, all subject matters need attention.

Perhaps the best way to teach time management is to be the example they need. Start young by having them have their own planner that is updated along with yours. This is an excellent way to start teaching common sight-words to preschoolers. Let them observe you planning weekly meals before going to the grocery store and laying out clothes for the next day. Eventually, the act of thinking ahead becomes second nature.

PLANNING, PRIORITIZATION, AND ORGANIZATION

Throughout childhood and adolescence, assignments, expectations, and life skills become increasingly complex and time-intensive. Many children, even those with advanced executive skills, benefit from additional instruction regarding planning, prioritization, and organization. Some extra time set aside to discuss goal-setting and how to achieve such goals would benefit any classroom and provide information that the child will utilize in all aspects of life for years to come. As we advance into the 21st century, these skills will become increasingly important. Every day we encounter massive amounts of information vying for our attention. This is just as true for children as it is for adults. Setting priorities and making plans to achieve goals is more important than ever in this often confusing world.

There is so much that can be taught simply by making it a part of the classroom structure. Not everything requires instruction in the form of a lesson plan. It's a good idea for teachers to have a classroom office set up so students can always find the materials they need to be successful. Paper, pens, highlighters, paper-clips, staplers, and anything else that is often used at school should be kept fully stocked and clearly labeled. Older elementary classrooms can even appoint an office monitor that ensures supplies are kept at an acceptable level. Of course, teachers can only do so much with the classroom budget allotted to them. Parents can be a big help by organizing fundraisers to help stock a successful classroom.

Early discussions about planning should revolve around simple activities that the child is accustomed to. By showing photos and asking for the kids to identify the most important aspect, the teacher accomplished two things. First, it allows the teacher to see and understand the point of view of each child. In addition, the teacher is able to visually explain why certain aspects are more important than others or must come first. Many kids are familiar with a peanut butter and jelly sandwich from the time they speak, so that could be a good way to start these conversations with youngsters. Have the child write instructions—if able—and check off items from the list as they go. This activity is useful throughout adolescence because it forces the child to closely consider an activity from all angles before setting out to tackle the problem. Also, discuss the most important steps in solving the problem. Consider what steps must be performed first, what steps rely on previous steps, and what steps need a bit more care and precision.

To-do lists are a necessary part of life, especially in the teenage years. Have the students keep daily, weekly, and monthly lists. Items should be highlighted or labeled to show the priority of each item on the lists. Allow the children to experiment with different methods of organization so they can find the best way for their individual minds. Some kids benefit from using different colored ink or highlighters to notate tasks with differing levels of importance, while others do well using sticky notes that can be moved to different calendars or moved to a completion list.

It's empowering to see their accomplishments pile up under the label *complete*. As with anything when dealing with children—or adults for that matter—examples really drive the point home and make the information easy to digest and comprehend. Have an easily accessible notebook filled with examples of to-do lists and step-by-step instructions that can serve as guides for the class. It's a good idea to allow students to add their own previously used and successful instructions to the notebook. Kids often enjoy sharing their discoveries with their peers.

Organization is so vital for success in school and in the years to come. Teachers should allow a few minutes during class to organize their materials and update their schedule. When done regularly, this shouldn't take away from usable instructional time. This time can also be used to discuss different organizational strategies for various areas of life. Ensure the classroom is neat and tidy, with a place for everything. The best way to teach is by example, so parents and teachers should try their best to keep their homes or classrooms well organized.

TASK LISTS

There are so many ways to organize tasks. Ensuring the right system is in place has a noticeably positive effect on performance. When thinking of a task list, what often comes to mind is the simple to-do list. This is just a holding area for ideas for all types of different tasks that need to be accomplished at some point in the future. This method is only the tip of the iceberg. Some people even find it helpful to create a NOT-to-do list. This is great for easily distracted or chronic procrastinators.

Charles M. Schwann, president of Bethlehem Steel Corporation, said the most profitable piece of advice he received was to make a daily to-do list in order of importance. Complete tasks in that sequence as time allows throughout the day. Many successful people still follow this advice, and it's a good idea to list items in order of importance, even if what works best is to accomplish them in a different order.

The ABC system is another popular way of managing tasks, and there are a couple of different ways to do this. Alan Lakein was a proponent of this technique in the 1970s. He made three separate lists: A, B, and C. List A contained the most important tasks, list C contained those of the lowest priority, and list B items fell somewhere in the middle. He would take it a step further by labeling each task A, B, and C in order of importance by numbers. Some people use this method by using list A for daily tasks, list B for weekly responsibilities, and list C for the monthly schedule. Many parents find it helpful to post a visual schedule of daily, weekly, and monthly tasks in some form or another.

Some people prefer to check the most unpleasant items off their list first. Energy levels, motivation, and patience are all at their highest levels first thing in the morning. This method takes away the excuse of not having the energy and putting it off for another day.

An occasional voice can be heard speaking against using task lists. Most of the reasons given for this stance are more applicable to adults, but some may apply to certain children as well. Some chronic procrastinators spend far too much time managing their lists—to the point of neglecting the implementation of them. This is referred to as *analysis paralysis*.

Ensure that some time is spent working on long-term goals. Quite often, tasks get rolled over from day-to-day, leading to a situation where only short-term plans are implemented. This may not matter much for young kids who don't often have very long-term goals, but it's a good idea to normalize working for something at a much later date. An adult who neglects their future plans in favor of immediate necessities would likely stay at a bad job for far too long.

HELPFUL TOOLS

"Easy to read" clocks should be everywhere and always show the correct time. State the time when starting or finishing the task. When getting started, give an estimate of how long a particular activity should take. Upon completion, once again note the time and compare how much time it actually took with the original estimate. Stopwatches are great for building time awareness because of their precision in measurement.

A favorite trick of parents everywhere who are trying to keep the household schedule running smoothly is a customized analog clock. There are a couple of ways to do this. Both methods can be a game-changer for young children, especially. The first method requires an analog clock with a light-colored face. Next, collect some magic markers (washable are best as the color will remain see-through and it can be easily wiped clean and reapplied when the schedule changes). Using different colors, mark the 'slices' of time meant for certain activities. For example, from 8:00 p.m. to 6:00 a.m. would be the same color to label the time for sleep.

The other way to use this method focuses on minutes, and it couldn't be any easier. Sticky notes or labels are used to notate what time something needs to be accomplished. If the goal is to leave home by 9:00am, about an hour before, put a sticky note at the 50-minute mark to put on shoes. Another sticky note at the 55-minute mark gives instructions to get into the car. These techniques are great not only for teaching kids how their days are ordered and what simple tasks actually encompass, but for getting them in the habit of keeping an awareness of time throughout the day.

The simple calendar is a must-have to consider long-term goals. It's easy to see major plans occurring throughout the year. The daily schedule can be written in ink or created on an electronic device through an application. The details needed on the daily schedule or task list can be as detailed as needed. Some kids will need every small step involved, such as getting their pen out and writing their name on the paper, to be spelled out clearly.

It really makes a big difference when school supplies and assignments stay organized. They should have a binder dedicated to each subject, color-coded if that makes it easier. Kids with executive function delays have a hard enough time with organization. This ensures their papers make it to the correct spot. Keep a three-hole-punch with reinforcing stickers handy in their backpack to ensure nothing gets lost or thrown away. Keep a small planner handy in the backpack to jot down anything that comes up during the day. The information can be transferred to a master planner at a later time. It's a good idea to keep both a paper and an online calendar so a backup is available against any technological or manual mishap that may damage the physical schedule.

It's often helpful to make things as visible as possible. Consider getting colorful lanyards for IDs and cards. They can be attached to the backpack to ensure they don't get lost or misplaced. A good, sturdy wallet will come in handy for older kids and teens. It should be able to hold everything and close easily, with plenty of room to spare. Set your child up for success in self-monitoring by providing the materials and resources necessary for them to learn.

8

SELF-MONITORING AND THE ROAD TO INDEPENDENCE

W hen considering the various executive functioning skills, self-monitoring is the supervisor. It is the ability to successfully manage oneself at an acceptable level in order to increase performance, motivation, and satisfaction. Someone with sound self-monitoring skills is aware of what is happening in their environment and within their bodies. Actions, behaviors, and even thoughts need to be controlled and reined in quite often throughout day-to-day life. This is an essential aspect of problem solving, while constant assessment determines how the activity is progressing. Actions that are working well will be continued, or even improved upon, while ineffective processes are altered or eliminated entirely.

It's important that children are encouraged to take responsibility for certain age-appropriate tasks starting in their toddler years. The parent should be present to point out the important aspects to remember, help along the way, and show how to determine if the activity was completed successfully and up to par. Once a skill is mastered and the child can accomplish it on their own, it's time for the parent to begin introducing the next activity. This not only helps to ensure the child grows up to be capable, but also gives a boost of motivation when there has been a constant string of challenges that have been consistently overcome.

When reviewing material for a test, it's helpful to teach students to use a color-coded highlighting system, which will help them pinpoint what they need help with. The material should be divided into three sections: material that is solidly understood, material they don't know well but have a plan to learn; and material that is completely unclear or confusing. Assign each section a different colored highlighter, as this makes it clear to the student and teacher where the confusion is.

It's advisable to check in with your child's self-monitoring skills, even if there are no noticeable executive functioning delays, as successful self-monitoring seems to be the bridge to adulthood. As the child gets older, they should be taught some simple self-monitoring techniques since so much happens during the school day. There are several simple ways for even young elementary children to effectively self-monitor. Ensuring directions are followed correctly is a simple and easy way to increase the quality of schoolwork. The child should reread the instructions after getting started and again after the work is completed. If there is any confusion regarding the directions, the teacher should be asked for clarification right away.

Working to increase reading comprehension will help tremendously in all subject areas. Depending on the child's comprehension level, have them stop every so often to check in with themselves and make sure they understand what they are reading. It's easy to go on auto-pilot, especially when it's been a long and busy day, so mechanisms should be put in place to prevent this from happening. There are no rewards for completing the assignment first, and often the most effective way to solve a problem is not always the most obvious. A bit of time in quiet contemplation before beginning work often leads to a more pleasant work experience and quite often ends up making work go more quickly anyway. Math isn't the only subject where there's a benefit to checking answers by working backwards. Word problems, history, and even writing can be improved by looking at the work in reverse order. Perhaps the most important thing to remember when building an effective self-monitoring system is to always be prepared for whatever may be required. For schoolchildren, this means their backpacks should be stocked with all the necessary materials and books. Many people find a checklist for each day of the week to be helpful. Review the list either before bed or in the morning to ensure a successful day.

Adults typically engage in self-monitoring instinctively and naturally, the process having become second nature after so many years of experience. Kids have a lot to learn about this subject, and the best teachers show by example. Monitor your progress out loud so the child is aware of important information to observe and learns that it's okay to change course when the activity is already underway. Children who have weak self-monitoring skills may exhibit the following behaviors:

- Unsure whether or not the directions are being followed correctly.
- Difficulty recognizing when they need help or asking for help.
- Don't understand words when they are used in a new and different context.
- Unaware if their answers make sense or not.

If your child is showing signs of weak skills, there is much that can be done to help the process along, both at home and with a licensed therapist. Cognitive behavioral therapists usually teach their clients some type of self-monitoring skills, and they have a wide array of techniques at their disposal. Each client is different and will require a fairly unique set of methods to see the best benefits from therapy. Usually, clients begin by journaling or checking in with themselves at certain times throughout the day. This is an effective method of data gathering. Later on, skills will be introduced to stop certain thoughts before they become problematic.

Self-monitoring is a part of nearly every activity, so it's important that children are given the proper tools and resources to develop the confidence and ability to accomplish their goals. These skills are vital in academic pursuits. Keeping track of assignments and schedules requires an increasing amount of responsibility throughout the school years. Mathematical skills benefit greatly from the ability to keep track of complex equations and consider different methods of solving the problem. Learning to read is an exercise in self-monitoring as words are sounded out to see if they resemble a known word. This process is called 'decoding.' After the written language has been decoded and understood, it's important to provide plenty of help to ensure the child begins to read for comprehension. Teach the child to stop periodically while reading to ask themselves questions, such as:

- What do I hope to learn from reading this?
- Do I understand the words, or do I need to use a dictionary?
- Do I understand the format—list, alphabetical order, or chapter—of the information?
- Does this relate to anything I already know?

Many emotions, behaviors, thoughts, and body feelings precede negatively patterned and recurrent thoughts or behaviors. A therapist will help identify the first warning signs that a downward spiral is beginning. It's much easier to halt such behavior at the beginning of the process. The simple act of monitoring thoughts, emotions, and actions can often lead to massive changes in behavior and attitude within a short time frame as unseen behavior and thoughts are physically recorded. The major purpose of these exercises is to bring awareness to how thoughts affect feelings of well-being and the overall experience of life.

OBSERVATION

At this stage, the child begins to gain an awareness of their thoughts, actions, and behaviors, and starts to understand the way these traits interact with each other. They are able to understand what is wanted from them in different situations and are aware if they often fall short of those expectations. Interrupting and talking over others is a bad habit that teachers and parents alike are constantly trying to stop. It is rude to others and prevents the child from learning as much as they could. One having success in the observation stage may catch themselves just as they are about to speak out in excitement and wait for a better time to contribute. This requires that they understand what the appropriate behaviors are in specific situations. It's also important that they begin to understand the emotions and thoughts that precede problematic behavior and learn to pick up on such red flags. Many students struggle with this skill as it takes quite a bit of reflection and self-awareness.

Autonomously monitoring behavior is an advanced executive functioning skill that may not be mastered until adulthood. Continue working with the child to uncover the hidden signs that indicate an impending negative thought or action. Eventually, everything will begin to come together and make sense. The skill of self-monitoring is one of metacognition, which is the ability to plan for and execute a task while monitoring themselves and the situation around them, determining problems, paying attention, and completing the task.

RECORDING

This is more than simply an awareness of behavior. The recording phase of self-monitoring serves to implement changes to behavior. Written records of certain occurrences allow patterns to be extracted so a truly actionable plan may be implemented. How long did the episode last? Where did it happen? What happened immediately before? Journaling is beneficial in this phase as there is a remembrance of prior situations, space for feelings to arise, and a choice to make corrections. An example of a simple journaling exercise that can be employed at this time can be seen below.

Situation	Thoughts	Emotions and Body Feelings	Response
Forgot about a history test tomorrow, and there's already a lot of homework tonight	I will never get everything done	Heart-racing, surprised, scared	Breathing exercise and homework, received a B on the test

The benefits of recording cannot be overstated. Self-monitoring quickly starts to become an unconscious behavior, especially in activities that are very familiar. Having written notes of certain behaviors—along with important contextual information—makes it easy to spot patterns and plan to make changes. It's also easier to implement strategies to address emotional, attentional, and self-regulation needs before a small hiccup becomes problematic. Checklists, parent/teacher/student communication sheets, journaling, and self-graphing are all good ideas to try out with your child to see what methods work best for them.

HOW TO SELF-MONITOR

Sometime around middle school, kids will be expected to take on more responsibilities for themselves in all areas of life. It can be confusing for them because, at some point, they will simply be expected to act in a particular way rather than being told what to do. There are various methods and techniques that are simple to understand, implement, and use. Take the child's lead in determining what type of scaffolding would be most beneficial. Don't allow reminders to become distracting and overshadow the task itself. Try two or three techniques, and rotate them with new methods if necessary.

Lists and reminders are helpful for both an overview of the big picture and for individual tasks. Goal-setting is a wonderful activity to do as a family. Revisit the goals every month or so to check progress and re-evaluate academic and social aspirations. Practice makes perfect, and role-playing is often the perfect opportunity for kids and teens to test out any situation, action, or reaction while in a safe environment. Teaching kids to watch—and sometimes mirror—other children while completing an activity can give valuable information when coaching and verbal explanations don't cut it. It's not always advisable to follow the crowd, but it's always a good idea to understand *how* the crowd behaves. Family and private journaling, combined with positive self-talk, can be beneficial when programming the mind for success. Many improvements can be seen by simply having a better outlook.

There are numerous techniques available to increase self-monitoring skills, and most kids see improvements fairly quickly when the right methods are employed. The main goal in teaching this skill set is for the child to move away from a situation where a parent or teacher monitors their progress so they can begin to take on the responsibility themselves. This won't happen overnight, and it won't happen in every aspect of life simultaneously. However, targeting certain activities and behaviors allows the lessons learned to spill over into other areas of life once a bit of confidence is gained.

Define Behavior(s) to Self-Monitor

Choose a behavior that is desired to increase, such as helping friends, turning assignments in on time, listening to instructions, or completing reading assignments. Behaviors that should decrease can also be monitored. Disrupting class, daydreaming during group work, rough actions with siblings, or not completing homework assignments are behaviors that can be monitored for extinction.

The child should always be aware of what behavior is being monitored, and what they can do to achieve success. Nobody likes to feel as if they are unknowingly being watched, and kids are no exception. Results are improved when the child understands the program and what is happening. It's important they understand exactly how to achieve their self-monitoring goals.

Choose a Method of Recording

Some children do just fine with mental checklists or other unwritten methods of self-monitoring. However, it's best for children who struggle in this area to keep written records. This allows patterns to become apparent to both the child and the teacher or parent, which leads to increased success. Some methods of recording are as follows:

- **Rating scale**: With this technique, kids rate themselves on how well they did in certain tasks such as staying in their seat, completing assignments, or raising their hand to speak. The child will give themselves a rating of poor, fair, or good at the end of the day or during other checkpoints throughout the day.
- **Checklist**: By writing out every step of a particular task, and having the child physically check off every item after its completion, certain activities quickly become second

nature. For example, a work readiness checklist may
consist of items such as: 1) Has all materials ready 2)
Workspace is organized 3) The directions are understood.

- **Frequency count**: This method of frequency counting is
purely informative. It tracks the number of times a certain
activity takes place. If Susan is working on paying
attention, she may keep a running tally of how many
times she catches herself lost in a daydream or gazing out
the window. There is no punishment or reward for
attaining a certain count, this is simply to bring awareness
to an issue and uncover patterns.

Choose a Schedule

It's important that the act of monitoring tasks does not end up
overshadowing the actual work being accomplished. Scaffolding in
any area should be complementary and not overpowering or stressful. Keeping up with detailed records at all times throughout the
day is difficult, so pick specific times to engage in self-monitoring
record keeping. Some children prefer to perform self-monitoring
checks before and/or after school, while others may prefer them
before and/or after an activity. It depends on the schedule and
temperament of the child, as well as the type of check being
performed. There could also be scheduled times throughout the
day to stop and record observations.

Decide on a Monitoring Cue

There often needs to be some sort of cue to remind the student
that it's time to check in with themselves to monitor their behavior.
This can be done in various ways and does not have to be
distracting to any of the students. Some commonly used monitoring cues are:

- **Beep tape**: This is a recording that plays a non-distracting tone at regular intervals to serve as a reminder to complete whatever self-monitoring technique is being practiced. Schools are able to download beep tapes with differing intervals, free of charge, at *www.interventioncentral.org/free-audio-monitoring-tapes*

- **Timer**: A simple kitchen timer or stopwatch is a great way to set reminders to check-in from time to time while doing homework. This performs much the same way as a beep tape, but tends to be easier for longer interval periods.

- **Teacher delivered cue**: Sometimes the teacher should check in with students by listing tasks that the students should be doing to stay on track. This can happen at the beginning, end, or at any time during self-led work.

- **Student delivered cues**: It's often best to allow the student to decide when to monitor their progress. Not everyone is at a good stopping point at the same time, especially for complex assignments. The teacher could ask their students to check-in three times while working, but it's up to the student to determine the time that happens.

Choose Rewards

A teacher or parent may want to give a reward for improved self-monitoring skills, although this is completely optional. It's not always a good idea to offer rewards to only some students in a classroom setting. As the child gets older, they should become more intrinsically motivated, rather than driven by reward. If you choose to offer rewards, keep in mind that not all rewards offer the same level of motivation to all students. Give rewards that really mean something to the child. You can get an idea about what motivates a child simply by watching them as they go about their day. What do they like to spend their time doing? A student who enjoys spending time with their best friend might be offered free-time with a friend during the final period, while the animal-loving student would like to have extra time to feed and play with the class pet. Surveying both the students and those close to them is another good way to create a personalized rewards system.

Create your own customizable rewards survey at: *www.intervention station.org/teacher-resources/student-rewards-finder*

Conduct Accuracy Checks

From time to time, the parent or teacher should check the self-monitoring reports for accuracy. It brings more self-awareness to the child when they are able to have an objective set of eyes on their behavior, and it's especially important to conduct such checks during the beginning of the self-monitoring journey.

Fade the Self-Monitoring Plan

The need for these practices will gradually start to fade over time. These processes do not need to be stopped at one time, but they can become simplified and gradually eliminated. This can be a tricky time, as the student is just beginning to truly stand on their own, but it's often very empowering when it becomes apparent how far they have come. The goals of the extinction processes are to simplify and streamline these practices so they are less intrusive and more sustainable over a long period of time, as well as to maintain any gains experienced by the student during this process. Instead of following a detailed checklist of every item on the morning to-do list, the list could be simplified or even reduced to a single reminder to make sure they are ready for school.

Behavior Charts

This method works particularly well in a classroom environment, but it's customizable nature also makes it a nice addition to work being done at home. Each student will be given a chart (shown below) with a list of both positive and negative behaviors. The teacher sets a timer for a certain number of minutes, and when the timer is up, each student records what behaviors they are engaging in at that moment. At this point, the students are not expected to monitor their behavior all the time, only in those specific moments when the timer dings.

	Period 1	Period 2	Period 3	Period 4	Period 5
Talking					
Out of seat					
Daydreaming					
Unkind words					
Causing distractions					
Aggressive					
Work turned in late					
Giving 100% effort					
Helping others/ sharing					
Reading					
Listening					
Assignments turned in on time					
Organized desk/supplies					
Conscientious					

This simple chart can be used in a variety of ways. After being introduced to and practicing the concept of monitoring at the buzzer only, have the child report what activities they engaged in between the dings of the timer. They can even rate their actions on a predetermined scale. Remember that this activity only concerns observing and recording the behaviors. Do not punish or reward students based on their self-reported conduct cards. It could lead to dishonesty and goes against the real purpose of this activity. If a child reports they were running in the hallway, thank them for the good job of being honest and asked how they should have made their way down the hallway.

This method is incredibly effective, as it really serves to improve behavior very quickly when used in conjunction with teaching self-management skills. Originally used as a time-saving technique by clinicians in gathering data for large groups, it soon became apparent that behavior improves rather drastically when it is systematically observed. It's also a good way for the whole class to discuss ways to manage their behavior as a whole. Although the teacher should never change what a student has reported, they may ask another student to verify the behavior of a classmate from time-to-time. Eventually, the students themselves may take over the behavior check discussions. It's advisable to have some ground rules put into place before letting the class fully self-monitor. Unless a child is at risk of causing physical harm, do not tattle at behavior checks. A compliment or two should also be given prior to discussing negative aspects of their behavior.

DEVELOPING SELF-MONITORING SKILLS

It's important to make the development of this skill a common topic of conversation, especially when discussing anything related to school or any specific goal. Even children who have strong skills in this area can benefit from some additional encouragement.

Journaling is a wonderful way for children to self-monitor that doesn't feel like schoolwork. By going back and re-reading journal entries; patterns, problems, and possible solutions that were previously hidden can suddenly become glaringly obvious. Social stories are a great way for parents and teachers to introduce kids to a new environment or task before they jump in with both feet. This is also a good way to make a point with a sensitive student that has a hard time taking corrections. Looking at an assignment from the teacher's point of view, or viewing the playground from another student's perspective, these are valuable lessons for all areas and times of life. Developing a sense of empathy helps us understand what is expected in various environments.

Many tools are available to help students with this process. Time-management logs compare how the student *should* spend their time with how that time is actually spent. The time period can be daily, weekly, or even for each individual activity. Checklists and rubrics give an objective measure of success in meeting expectations and goals. It's also rewarding to check off completed work. Signing contracts or agreements can be beneficial because it gives the task a grown-up feel and adds an extra level of accountability. This works even better when the child is in on creating the agreement. Rating scales give students the opportunity to rate themselves, and this usually works better when it is kept private, at least after the process is understood. Behavior report cards are most beneficial when completed by both the teacher and student because it gives an idea of what areas the student may be experiencing struggles that they are not aware of themselves.

This is a work-in-progress, even throughout adulthood. As roles and responsibilities change, so too must the methods used, as well as the intensity of those methods to self-monitor. By making this skill a regular talking point and offering a variety of techniques to hone this skill, parents and teachers can set the next generation up for both academic and personal success.

9

DEALING WITH TRANSITIONS

I t's true that children are resilient, but that doesn't mean change comes easily to them. Transitions are especially challenging for children with executive functioning delays since their lives are generally very methodical to ensure success. A time period that's difficult for all with executive challenges is the transition from elementary to middle school. This is a very formative period; they are no longer little kids but on their way to their teenage years. The instructional format is now completely different and the educational demands are vastly more complex and demanding.

The elementary school atmosphere was very controlled. One or two teachers in one or two classrooms was the extent of the learning environment. Assignments were short-term and progress was reviewed by the teacher constantly. Now in middle school, there are many teachers with many personalities. Every class has a different personality with different students. At the same time, the structure of the educational experience transforms, and the difficulty level of the work increases dramatically. There are long-term projects that require a great deal of planning, and nobody is standing over their shoulder to make sure they progress. If a child's lack of executive aptitude went unnoticed in elementary school, it will surely become apparent now.

Each skill seems to be tested to the max at this time. An increased workload demands more from their working memory. Long-term projects require planning and organization. Changing social demands necessitate more self-control. All of these simultaneous changes often push their developing, and already struggling, executive skills too far. The most important thing parents can do is maintain an awareness of the executive skill level during this transition period, offering help and guidance as needed. Parents who have been working on these skills previously will need to re-evaluate their plans and methods. It's natural to want to protect your already struggling child during this time, but the experience of independence at this stage is critical.

This doesn't mean it isn't necessary to remain a solid supporter with elevated levels of assistance. Unfortunately, the middle-school transition often serves as an amplifier for children who are already at risk for poor outcomes, although those who deal with this particular transition in a positive way can change their trajectory for the better. Many factors make up a successful middle school transition, including:

- maturity level
- coping skills
- characteristics of the new school environment
- level of preparation
- support available before, during, and after the transition
- the child's perception of the changes

- the match between the new environment and their developmental needs

Parents of kids with executive delays may not need to hold their hands so tightly now, but their success going forward in life depends on having a bit of help navigating this new, grown-up world.

PREPARING FOR THE CHANGE

There's a lot that you can do as a parent that will make this time as easy as possible. This subject should be a frequent topic of conversation in the months leading up to the transition into middle school. Talk about how classes are set up and what types of projects are in store, being sure to answer any questions they might have. Start the conversation early so there is ample opportunity for them to ask questions as they gain a better understanding of what is to come.

By now, most children with executive function challenges are well aware of the difficulty they have with changes and how confusing it is to start something new. Get familiar with the drive there. Make note of how long it will take to arrive in rush hour traffic. Every new discovery should initiate a conversation. Now that the length of the car ride is known, it's time to start discussing when a proper wake-up and bedtime would be. Keep in mind that telling a child what is going to happen does not constitute a discussion. When they are provided with the proper information and approached as a decision maker, you may be surprised at the mature response.

The school will surely help parents plan practice runs at the school. Visit the locker to practice locking and unlocking it; walk to all classes in order; visually note the location of important offices; go to the cafeteria and take a look at a sample menu. Throughout their lives, the most important factor for these kids has been practice. Trial runs serve as practice for some of the things that may cause undue stress, which takes away from the educational experience. Manipulating a combination lock is a new technique for both the mind and hands. Maybe it would be a good idea to purchase one several months before school starts. This way, fumbling fingers won't threaten the child with a tardy or incomplete homework assignment.

Talk about potential challenges and the many aspects of school life that will be changing. Have the children help in developing a plan to stay on track. The method of scheduling will need to be updated since the demands will be so vastly different. Many students find it helpful to keep a planner at school to jot any notes down, and get assistance from their parents in ensuring the information is transferred to the master planner correctly.

Some families benefit from setting up a scheduling day to plan for the following week. For example, Sunday evening would be an excellent time to take a look at projects and assignments with various due dates. Daily homework assignments usually take a consistent amount of time, so work together in order to schedule time to prepare and polish long-term projects. Scheduling should be done in a way that makes the process easy to understand and implement, with sufficient help in determining the correct order for all steps involved.

NEW BEGINNINGS

While the first few months in a new environment can leave anyone feeling like a fish out of water, some difficulty adjusting can be normal while adjustments are made. However, it's vital to pay attention to concerns about changes in behavior that persist over the long term. Depression and anxiety may often manifest at this point. Many adults don't think such young children could feel depressed or anxious, but the experience of so many changes happening at once can be quite troubling for anyone, regardless of age. Such mood disorders severely interfere with executive functioning skills, so it's imperative to seek help before the child falls behind. Many times, these issues can be resolved by therapy and the introduction of coping mechanisms. Situational depression and anxiety do not have to be lifetime sentences if dealt with promptly and correctly.

Organization is the cornerstone of a successful transition into middle school. Introduce a color coding system as supplies are prepared. Designate a different color for each subject for binders, folders, or even pens to write assignments and schedule blocks in their planner. Doing so turns the very complex mental task of juggling different responsibilities in different places into something that can be physically seen.

Don't worry too much about helicopter parenting at this point. The first half of sixth grade requires parents to stay on top of everything and ensure assignments are done correctly and on time. Independence can come later for children who do well at managing the change. If problems manifest early on, there will need to be a greater level of parental involvement and possibly psychological intervention. It can seem hard to know when to seek outside help, but psychologist Kevin Kemelhar has an early warning sign to look out for, "The red flag is when you and your spouse start to argue over your kid's homework" (Wismer, 2022).

Reaching out to the teacher is the first step in navigating this rough terrain. Middle school teachers have seen issues with adjusting manifest in a myriad of ways. They have lots of tricks up their sleeves that make a difference for harder-to-reach students. Minor difficulties with executive function can often be fixed simply by bringing the issue to the teacher's awareness.

Checking-In

While everything settles into a new normal and the child seems to be doing well, there will still be work to be done. From this point forward, social and academic pressures will constantly increase. It's easy to miss early signs of trouble in the hectic life of a modern family.

Keep an eye on school supply levels and ensure they are kept in a known location. The world of a middle and high school student is action-packed and fast-paced. Even the most organized child may forget to tell a parent when they are running short on paper. It's a good idea to meet with teachers as early in the semester as possible. Bring up any concerns and make the teacher aware of any strengths or weaknesses. They do not wish to make a child uncomfortable among their peers and will resist calling on them for an answer on such a subject until the material is learned.

Make it a point to have academic check-ins with the child periodically throughout the semester. Be aware of any large projects and the due dates to ensure work is being accomplished in a steady manner. Over the years, methods used for organizing and planning will need to be altered. This is often a sign that new educational and executive skill levels are coming online. It's helpful to have parental involvement when a new major step is underway.

10

DEALING WITH FRUSTRATIONS

Many parents are surprised by how moody their children with poor executive functioning skills can be. The moods can come out of nowhere and seem out of character because, overall, many of these kids are quite easygoing. Their frustrations stem from an inability to function in the same way as their peers and the lack of results they see in comparison. The feelings of overwhelm can grow rapidly, possibly leading to giving up altogether. Parents and teachers are often frustrated by a seemingly flippant attitude, but the children experiencing delays are more aware of the troubles this issue causes than anyone.

Give some grace and understand if your child has an attitude at times. That's wonderful. It means the child is completely normal. Life is hard, and it's even harder with a lack of knowledge, experience, and freedom. Someone with executive delays will likely be more frustrated than others because they experience quite a bit more difficulty throughout their days. If a sour mood persists, try to uncover the root cause and determine if there is a solution.

When children are approached in a kind and helpful manner, they are more likely to open up about the source of their frustrations.

MENTAL WELLNESS

Always practice mental wellness and teach mental coping mechanisms as the child grows. When their capabilities are called into question for a new and complicated task, pep talks can do wonders for self-esteem. Positive statements give the confidence needed to take that all-important first step, and good choices come from high levels of self-confidence.

Stress is creeping into the lives of our children at younger and younger ages. Stress is linked to both depression and anxiety. Stress essentially freezes the executive functioning capabilities in children. Be proactive as middle school begins and during busy times of heightened activity. Introducing meditation and practicing mindfulness techniques brings the center of attention back to the present moment and away from the many demands of the future. Breathing exercises, gratitude journals, body scanning, and acts of kindness create a strong, positive mindset that will take the child far in life. The benefits of such simple activities cannot be overstated. Greater focus, reduced anxiety, increased working memory, and greater impulse control are seen in schoolchildren who practice mindfulness techniques.

PHYSICAL ACTIVITY

Daily exercise is so important for the mental and physical health of children, especially those who present with ADHD symptoms. It seems they have to 'buy' focus by using all of their extra energy. Ensuring they get enough movement on a daily basis keeps their tanks full. Physical activity is crucial in getting blood and oxygen flowing to the brain. Individual activities, like yoga, are helpful in bringing an immediate, needed dose of calming energy, while team sports and group activities, like soccer and martial arts, hold other benefits. Group exercise not only gives a boost of endorphins, it also encourages strategy, adaptability to the actions of others, and self-monitoring behavior.

Brain plasticity is a major factor in how well an individual learns and remembers. This means the brain is able to change its focus quickly when presented with a range of stimuli. Exercise is one of the easiest and best ways to enjoy the increased brain plasticity that is so beneficial to a successful educational experience. Exercise teaches the brain to communicate with itself more efficiently, and this carries into all the other areas of life.

Endorphins and endocannabinoids are released into the bloodstream during and following an intense bout of physical exertion. Such chemicals are vital components of a balanced mood and a positive mental state. This is important in a learning environment, of course, but such a state is crucial in building and maintaining healthy relationships. Children prone to emotional outbursts often struggle with making friends; exercise ensures they are in the proper mental state to build friendships among their peers.

Moving into the future, the next generations will likely spend a lot of time using devices that manage and drive their lives. Setting up good routines around exercise is now more important than ever. Kids who exercise regularly are generally less aggressive, less anxious, less depressed, and experience fewer social difficulties.

SIP ON SUGAR

Many children who struggle with the symptoms of ADHD likely have a special diet that reduces sugar intake, as sweets can have a particularly negative effect on them. Frequent sweet treats for no reason have a negative impact on memory. However, when a child is doing mentally demanding work, like a science project or sitting for a long standardized exam, it's a good idea to sip on a sugary drink. The sugar in liquid form serves to give the quick boost of extra energy needed to push through a tough task. This increases the blood glucose levels just enough to get the job done without derailing a carefully planned diet.

PERSONAL DRIVE

Self-evaluation is a key part of practicing successful executive functioning skills, but this ability does not always manifest without help from parents and caregivers. When a situation goes badly, get in the habit of calmly asking questions such as:

- How do you think it went?
- What could be done differently next time?
- What skills could be improved upon before the next game/meet/test?
- What did you learn from the disappointment?
- How are you feeling about the disappointment?

Doing this in a calm way destigmatizes failure and allows it to be turned into a valuable learning opportunity. People who do not let small setbacks annoy them have high levels of resilience. This increases opportunities and chances for overall success. Let the child see that effort is what matters in shaping intelligence and experiencing success. Those who believe in the power of effort over natural talent are more likely to learn from mistakes and take chances that pay off.

Resilience starts with talk and comments from the parents. Pay attention to the ways praise and criticism are phrased. There's nothing to be gained from praising a natural trait such as general intelligence by saying, "You're so smart!" Instead, complement an accomplishment by saying something like, "I'm so proud of you for completing the whole essay alone." By the same token, criticism needs to be targeted; the phrase, "I'm so disappointed in you," does nothing to identify the problem or propose solutions. It's preferable to say something like, "I know this grade is disappointing. I hope you come to me for help next time you get stuck." This separates the disappointment from the child and offers a solution when a similar problem arises.

Setbacks and failure are a part of life for everyone, even the most successful leaders. Don't insulate the child from this experience; instead, teach them how to move forward in a calm and empowered manner. This is the ultimate skill in life.

11

HELPFUL RESOURCES

When problems needing outside intervention become apparent, it's difficult to know where to turn. Those exhibiting executive dysfunction need help right away. Falling behind during such formative years, both academically and socially, can be detrimental to long-term well-being. There are many ways to address problems, and the methods used will depend entirely upon the individual child. Sometimes there is a period of trial and error while the family determines what works, but after a successful management plan has been found, there will only be minor adjustments needed over time. This chapter outlines all of the resources available for assistance during uncertain times.

EXPERTS

Dealing with executive delays is a confusing time for everyone involved. Most mental and developmental disorders affect some or all executive skills, and it's possible to experience dysfunction in this area with no concurrent disability or disorder. It can take an assortment of medical professionals practicing in different settings to get a true picture of what's going on. Stay positive throughout the process of discovery. The caregiver orchestrating the intervention has a wonderful opportunity to be an exemplary example of strength and stability in times of uncertainty.

Physical Therapists

When improvement in range of motion, pain management, or the introduction of a healthy lifestyle is needed, physical therapists are first on the list to call. They can help children with executive delays gain an awareness of their bodies, which promotes independence. Sometimes, executive dysfunction is a result of a brain injury. In such cases, there will certainly be a need for physical therapy.

Movement plays a big role in executive skills, especially in children. So many activities, even many that take place in school, involve some sort of physical motion. Major problems can sometimes be solved by correcting a minor movement. For example, a severe dislike of writing is caused by something as simple as an incorrect pencil grip.

Occupational Therapists

Occupational therapists help patients master daily life skills. They do this by focusing on the physical body, the mind, and sensory input. These professionals work with those of a wide range of abilities and assist with an assortment of daily tasks. They do it all, from getting bathed and dressed in the morning, to creating a functional work environment. There are many reasons why a person may need help doing things like managing time, budgeting, grocery shopping, and doing household chores. Occupational therapists will assist in assessing your child's strengths and weaknesses and are skilled in working with those who have learning disabilities or mood disorders. Collaboration between the occupational therapist and the teacher is monumental in reaching difficult students as they both have so much knowledge to offer regarding a conducive work environment.

During a session, the child will be made to feel right at home. The therapist might ask them to join in on some activities, like catch or role-play, to act out certain situations. As the sessions continue, they will start working on more complex skills during their time. Making a schedule to improve time management or practicing handwriting may be some of the things the therapist wishes to observe. They may even test the child for a sensory processing disorder, which often occurs along with ADHD. Kids who have trouble processing sensory stimuli are not the same at all. The condition can manifest as an inability to slow down as well as excessive daydreaming.

Speech-Language Pathologist

Many children need some help with learning to communicate effectively. Communication, both verbal and non-verbal, is a major part of executive functioning. Without the skills to understand instructions or communicate needs, it's difficult to be in command of one's life. Speech therapy not only teaches children how to put thoughts into words, it also teaches when it's appropriate to say those words. Situational awareness is a big part of speech therapy, and understanding such connections often makes a big difference in the amount and type of communication. A speech language pathologist can help in the following ways:

- Teach students to "read the room" by paying attention to the time, place, and people.
- Encourage self-directed speech as a method to drive thoughtful and intentional decisions.
- Work together to think through problems and ideas.

- Help make backup plans.

Speech therapy is especially useful for children with an ADHD diagnosis. This type of therapy is not only about language coming from kids, it is also about ensuring the information received by the child is accurate. Taking in excess sensory information means that a little extra help is needed to filter and decipher mental input. Sometimes, melt-downs are easily avoided when the child correctly understands a particular situation.

Developmental and Behavioral Pediatricians

These doctors specialize in children who are not developing at a normal rate due to learning disabilities and/or behavioral issues. They are important in diagnosing complex issues like ADHD, ODD, or autism in children, as the symptoms can point to more than one possible diagnosis and can get rather confusing. Some of the things they will watch out for that can point to a developmental issue are:

- delayed speech
- delayed motor abilities
- trouble learning age-appropriate information
- social difficulties
- school performance

They determine the existence, or extent, of an issue in a variety of ways and pull information from many sources. These doctors will likely gather information using the following methods:

- performing a medical exam
- gathering medical history
- observation

- talking with the child
- asking the parents about behavior in various settings
- feedback from teachers at school or daycare

In some cases, developmental and behavioral pediatricians may seek collaboration with other specialists, such as occupational or speech therapists. Concerning symptoms do not always coincide with an official diagnosis. Developmental and behavioral pediatricians are of great assistance to families in such a confusing time.

THERAPIES

Numerous therapies are available for the treatment and resolution of issues resulting from weak executive skills—such as speech or occupational therapy—but one of the most beneficial types of therapy for these kids is cognitive behavioral therapy. This therapy can be applied in many different life situations and is easily tailored to the needs of the child. Because executive functioning issues can occur in a wide variety of life situations, a wide range of therapies may be recommended by the child's primary pediatrician or psychologist. The therapy and/or medication regimen is not set in stone. It's understood that such programs are fluid in nature and will be revisited and revised often.

Cognitive Behavioral Therapy

This is a form of talk therapy that is typically used short-term. Results are usually seen within a few months, and sometimes, major improvements occur after just a few weeks. Cognitive behavioral therapists seek to change an existing negative thought pattern into a positive one, thus affecting emotions and actions. They deal with a wide range of issues from individuals of varying abilities, so they have many techniques in their repository.

- **Cognitive restructuring**: The therapist will ask about the thought process in certain situations and can help identify problematic patterns. Assuming the worst will happen can sometimes become a self-fulfilling prophecy. Instead of worrying about the essay because she always performs poorly on written assignments, Alice learns to think in a way that appreciates the work she has put into her writing. This gives her the confidence to get started right away, which is the best way to guarantee success.

- **Guided discovery**: Once the therapist acquaints themselves with the patient's viewpoint, they will ask for evidence in support of and against that point of view. This opens different perspectives, allowing for new choices. Perhaps Alice thinks that the group of children she wants to play with don't like her. The therapist will then ask how she knows this and explain that just because somebody doesn't approach her does not mean she dislikes her. Over time, Alice understands the opposing point of view and works up the courage to approach the children, and making new friends.

- **Exposure therapy**: This method is used to confront and extinguish fears and phobias. This is done in a way that doesn't provoke undue anxiety. The therapist will be there to provide help with practicing coping mechanisms, and it will be done incrementally. Some highly sensitive children are very reactive to loud noises, the sound is amplified to them. By exposure to the source of the discomfort in a controlled method, usually building up to the full intensity, the therapist seeks to lessen the harsh physiological response to the stimuli.

- **Journaling**: This practice can be used in various ways and is a great technique to use personally throughout life.

The therapist may like the patient to use journaling as a way to track the progress of new thoughts and behaviors.

- **Activity scheduling**: Some people with executive dysfunction will put off undesirable activities indefinitely. The therapist helps in implementing a plan and setting a start date. Plus, having someone aware of and actively working on the issue with the patient adds a sense of accountability.

- **Behavioral experiments**: This is common with anxiety disorders and catastrophic thinking. The therapist will ask for a prediction before beginning an activity that leads to anxiety. Afterwards, the prediction is compared with the results, showing that the catastrophe is not likely to happen. Alice may have thought that the children would make fun of her if she approached them. She is sure to see that after practicing other methods to change her mindset and help her gain confidence—the results will not be what she thought. She may even make a whole new group of friends.

- **Relaxation**: Ways to manage stress are learned, often through techniques such as deep breathing exercises, imagery, and progressive muscle relaxation. The therapist may use guided meditation as a way to positively influence the mindset during such activities.

- **Role-playing**: Acting out certain scenarios can help with gaining familiarity with certain atmospheres, reducing anxiety in social situations, helping with practicing assertiveness, and improving communication skills. It's also helpful to have kids act out opposing roles to get an idea of why their parents or teachers act a certain way or have certain rules. The therapist may have Sam pretend to be his mom as she tries—often unsuccessfully—to wake him up for school. The ordeal feels different when he is in the position of having to get something accomplished, while someone else was less than helpful.

- **Successive approximation**: The therapist helps break down complex tasks into small steps. A final history project is broken down into small steps to be accomplished week-by-week, making the finished project come together easily.

Medications

Medication may be needed to control symptoms that interfere with learning and social interactions. ADHD is the primary coexisting disorder that may require medication for some period of time. The child's medical team may prescribe stimulant, non-stimulant, or antidepressant medication. Often, problems that are corrected early do not require constant medication. It's important to take the exact dose prescribed by the doctor, and do not stop any medication without prior discussion with the doctor.

- **Stimulant medication**: These are used to control impulsivity, short attention span, and hyperactivity. Between 70–80% of children with ADHD experienced reduced symptoms under a regimen that included these medications (Bhandari, 2021). Stimulants increase dopamine and norepinephrine levels in the brain, allowing extra energy, better attention, and mental alertness. Commonly prescribed and recognized stimulant medications are Adderall, Dexedrine, ProCentra, Focalin, and Ritalin. Most brands are available in different formulations for short-acting, intermediate-acting, and long-acting results.

- **Non-stimulant medication**: Stimulant medications are often the first choice because of their effectiveness, but there are some unpleasant side-effects that may occur. In these cases, a non-stimulant may be prescribed in addition to, or instead of, the previously prescribed medication. Commonly used brands include Strattera, Kapvay, Intuniv, and Qelbree.
- **Antidepressants**: Antidepressants can be helpful, and some blood-pressure medications have a calming effect on hyperactive children.

EDUCATIONAL RESOURCES

Tools of the Mind

www.toolsofthemind.org

This curriculum is based on the teachings of Russian psychologist Lev Vygotsky. He believed that there are mental tools that enhance and expand our mental abilities just like the physical tools that increase our physical potential. He believed these mental tools needed to be mastered; doing so is just as important as learning facts. Until these mental tools are able to be used, a child's learning will be completely controlled by the surrounding environment. What is the loudest, brightest, most colorful object? That is where attention and, therefore, learning will occur. For something to be recorded into memory, it must be repeated multiple times. The International Bureau of Education named this curriculum "an exemplary educational intervention" (Tools of the Mind, 2020).

The methods used differ from those in a typical kindergarten environment in several ways. First, intentional theoretical performance is a major part of the plan. There are certain specific rules to play.

Props can be used, such as a block to symbolize a loaf of bread. Play is based on stories in books and literature rather than activities common in everyday life. The class begins with fairy tales but very quickly moves to chapter books. This method utilizes play to teach language skills, reading comprehension, vocabulary, and creativity.

Also, there is a substantial amount of scaffolding put into place by the teacher. Peer interaction and community-mindedness are a part of nearly all activities. Social intelligence, persistence, and the intrinsic desire to accomplish tasks are fostered in such an environment. A study in 2014 found this program to have a positive influence on reasoning ability, attention, reading comprehension, math, vocabulary, and overall executive functioning skills by the end of kindergarten and into first grade (Tools of the Mind, 2020).

The Pathway 2 Success Blog

www.thepathway2success.com

This in-depth resource center has numerous lesson plans, all with a focus on increasing executive functioning skill levels. Social Emotional Learning (SEL) is a unique curriculum that focuses on five major themes:

- self-awareness
- self-management
- social awareness
- relationships
- decision-making

Other lesson plans and activities that foster many skills relating to executive functioning are available on the website, such as those focusing on mindfulness and coping mechanisms. An archive of blog posts full of tips, tricks, lesson plans, and ideas is free to anyone browsing the site. There is also a members-only resource center with an entire library full of lessons and teaching materials.

Teachers Pay Teachers

www.teacherspayteachers.com

A fabulous, easy-to-use resource center for learning materials in every school subject. Books, games, worksheets, and study guides in language arts, foreign languages, math, science, history, social studies, art, and music for all grade levels can be ordered with ease.

The Child Mind Institute

www.childmind.org

This organization is serious about protecting the mental health of children. Those struggling with learning disorders, mental health issues, or traumatic events will find this resource center to be a good starting place. Information can be found on just about every subject dealing with children's mental health and education, and their team is eager to help point those in need of assistance in the right direction.

ADDitude Mag

www.additudemag.com

The go-to resource for everything you need to know about ADD. Symptom checkers, treatment information, learning tips, and much more can be found all in one place. It's easy to navigate to information that can have an impact on the life of a loved one. There are resources geared towards students, parents, teachers, and therapists.

Edutopia

www.www.edutopia.org

A fascinating library with an interesting history, full of unique ideas to create an environment conducive to learning. The visionaries at Edutopia see a future where social cooperation will be second nature to children who grow up in current times. Founded in the early 90s by filmmaker George Lucas, Edutopia focuses on several major understandings:

- comprehensive assessment
- integrated studies
- project-based learning
- teacher development
- technology integration

These areas of focus are just as important today as they were 30 years ago. Edutopia is sure to continue offering resources to educational leaders for years to come.

LD Online

www.ldonline.org

An extensive library on topics of importance to, and about, those with ADHD who also have learning disabilities. There is an extensive question and answer portion with topics that are often confusing to those just starting out on their journey. IEPs, early intervention, disability legislation, classroom accommodations, and homeschooling help are just some of the many topics this resource center can be of assistance in finding information about.

GAMES

Board games have been a mainstay of family nights for many years, and it's easy to see why. Following directions, taking turns, and planning strategies are lifelong skills that can and should be practiced in comfortable and fun environments. Although kids with executive functioning delays often struggle with these skills, these easy-to-learn games make listening and planning exciting. Be sure to point out what skills are being practiced and how they relate to everyday life.

- **Max (ages 4–7)**: Teaches emotional control, planning and prioritizing, and flexible thinking. It's a board game that requires cooperation from all players. A bird, a chipmunk, and a mouse are trying to escape from Max the cat. A roll of the dice determines how far the little animals can move, but the number of squares they may advance can be split between them. Kids learn to constantly change their strategy and look for new solutions.
- **AnimalLogic (age 5+)**: Teaches organization, flexible thinking, planning, and prioritization. There are varying levels of difficulty built into this game, ensuring it will grow along with your child and remain a favorite for years to come. Giraffes, camels, lions, and hippos need to cross a bridge, but they can only move in a particular order.
- **No Stress Chess (age 7+)**: Teaches planning, prioritization, task initiation, organization, flexible thinking, and impulse control. Even kids know chess as the ultimate strategy game that is difficult to master. For some, this complexity makes the idea of playing chess seem out of reach. *With No Stress Chess*, kids are given the rules as they play, allowing them to focus on the game itself rather

than memorizing the procedures. After a while, they will remember the rules and the game can be transformed into a standard chess game when they become comfortable with them.

- **Jenga (age 8+)**: Teaches self-monitoring, impulse control, and flexible thinking. A tall tower is constructed with each layer consisting of three blocks. The blocks are arranged in opposite positions on alternating layers. When it's their turn, each child selects one block to remove from the body of the tower and places it on the top layer. They must use careful planning and self-monitoring to continue without knocking the whole tower down.

- **Distraction (age 8+)**: Teaches flexible thinking and working memory. Kids won't even know they are challenging their working memory when enjoying an exciting game of Distraction. Each player draws a card that shows a number. Everyone must recite all numbers in order. It gets quite complicated after several players have a turn.

- **Quiddler (age 8+)**: Teaches planning, prioritization, organization, and flexible thinking. This is a fantastic spelling game, but unlike Scrabble, players win by spelling the highest number of small words.

- **Snake Oil (age 10+)**: Teaches task initiation, organization, and flexible thinking. This game is sure to be a welcome addition to any family's game night collection. There is a customer and a salesman. The customer draws a card describing who they are—rock star, doctor, teacher, etc.—while the other player draws a card with a word describing a product they will try to sell to their customer.

- **MindTrap (age 12+)**: Teaches flexible thinking. This is

a riddle game that can be played alone or in teams,
making it perfect for a child who enjoys word puzzles.

These games are tried and true favorites that have brought many
smiles and taught many lessons. Pick one up for the next family
night and see what good times will come. Detailed instructions for
each game can be found at *www.understood.org/articles/en/8-fun-
games-that-can-improve-your-childs-executive-functioning-skills*

APPS

There are many who follow the school of thought that electronics
and screen time are the root causes of delays in executive skills.
While this may or may not be the case, older children and teens
will be exposed to, and expected to use, electronics during their
educational experience. Teaching the proper use of technology and
showing how it can help in building a desired life experience will be
more beneficial long-term than avoidance. There have always been
countless productivity apps geared towards adults. Now these
helpful software applications are changing the lives and educational
experiences of children around the world. A quick search with
some keywords describing what you're looking for will show
numerous results, and there are many options that have a proven
track record of success.

Some of these apps do have a one-time fee or are subscription-
based, but most often there is a trial period to determine if it is
something that could work for your child.

- **Thinking Time Pro**: Perfect for preschoolers and
  kindergartners, this app has thoughtful games that stress
  memory, logic, impulse control, and flexibility. The games

may be difficult for young children to grasp, so be sure to set aside some time to help your kids get started with this playful learning app.

- **Choiceworks**: This visual scheduling app breaks down multi-step, complex tasks in an easy-to-understand manner. As a bonus, this game focuses not only on activities, like getting ready in the morning, but also teaches important social and behavioral lessons by showing how to calm down when upset.

- **Todo Telling Time**: An interactive game for children in kindergarten to second grade. It's a useful tool for helping them learn how to tell the time, understand how a calendar works, and start learning about a schedule's components.

- **First Then Visual Schedule HD**: A visual scheduling app that gives ordered instructions to help children learn certain routines such as bathtime, getting ready in the morning, or Saturday afternoon sports practices. Allow the child to choose the thumbnail picture and audio message, plus there is the option of adding a reward.

- **Goalbook Toolkit**: An app made specifically for teachers with many diverse learners in their classroom. It's a way to manage personalized goals with easy to find information about the current abilities of the child. This cuts down on paperwork and rummaging for information. There is a large database with information about different methods to teach certain materials, as well as methods to practice culturally responsive teaching.

- **Remind**: A messaging system meant for a class setting that became popular with the rise of remote learning. Send schedules, assignments, and reminders to the child and their family to ensure everyone stays on the same page. Teachers should be sure not to overuse messaging services, since most kids are inundated with information coming from many directions and can quickly become overwhelmed.

- **Time Timer**: A customizable stopwatch with the ability to have multiple timers for different activities simultaneously. The graphics are easy to read, and children can keep track of how much time they have spent on math homework, reading, chores, and playing on their tablet. Visually seeing their responsibilities and watching the progression towards completion is rewarding in itself.

- **WorkFlowy**: This clean, streamlined app is ideal for organizing notes, planning projects, managing task lists, and staying organized. The dashboard is not distracting, which is important for some neurodivergent children.

- **MindMeister**: This classroom sharing app makes sharing the syllabus and learning materials in an easy-to-find location for the whole class as easy as possible. There is also the option to allow students editing rights on certain portions. This allows for a consistently updated FAQ section of the class and gives a sense of community-mindedness and cooperation amongst the students.

- **iHomework 2**: A clean dashboard helps students quickly and easily track homework assignments, long-term projects, exams, and extra-curricular activities all in one place. The search tool makes it easy to find information quickly. The tasks option has an added layer of scaffolding support that helps the student understand how to break down complex assignments.

- **Bear**: This app is a dream for the up-and-coming writer. Text is brought to life in a way that is pleasing to the user, and ideas are easy to organize. Track word count, writing time, and reading time with user friendly tools. Many features are available on the free option, and all features of BearPro are unlocked with a one-time fee.

- **30/30**: The ultimate taskmaster, 30/30 helps users stay on a customized schedule and gives reminders to take regular breaks.
- **Quizlet**: Studying has never been easier with Quizlet. Use millions of flashcards uploaded by other students or create your own. Games keep the child's attention, while easy-to-use sharing tools help them stay connected with teachers and classmates.
- **YouNote!**: Take notes by writing, speaking, or even drawing. With YouNote!, students will be able to catch every word for easy review at a later time. It's easy to search by keyword and share with others.
- **InClass**: This app is for older kids, middle-schoolers, and all the way up to college students. It's simple and clean interface makes it easy to keep track of class times, homework assignments, and project due dates. Notes and audio files can be attached to notes, and helpful reminders keep users on track.
- **Bionic Reading**: This is a new application programming interface (API). It enhances reading skills by keeping the reader focused on the page. The ability to filter through large amounts will become more important as time goes on. The first few letters of the words are in bold, which acts as "fixation points," helping guide the reader effortlessly through the text. This may be a game changer for neurodivergent readers.

GOVERNMENT SUPPORT

All children are entitled to an appropriate and fair education. It's vital that plans are in place for students with disabilities or different educational needs. There are two types of educational plans meant to support children in their pursuit of an education: The 504 plan and the IEP. They both serve different purposes, and whichever one is the most helpful depends entirely on the child.

504 Plan

This plan is covered under the Rehabilitation Act and ensures that a person cannot be discriminated against because of a disability. The 504 plan is reviewed on an "as needed" basis, but the basic rule of thumb is every three years. To qualify, a person must have a disability that impacts at least one major life area in a substantial way. Students who benefit from such a plan need additional support or accommodations but not specialized instruction. Some examples of common accommodations are preferential seating, assistive technology, and receiving written instructions. There is no age limit with a 504 plan; it can even carry over into college.

Individualized Education Plan

All students who require special education are entitled to certain classroom accommodations or allowances. An individualized education plan (IEP) is a legal document outlining the specific abilities and needs of a child. It's updated regularly and must include three components. The first part of the IEP outlines how the child is now: Their current strengths, weaknesses, and needs. Next, the document lays out concrete goals that are challenging, yet attainable. This portion needs to be very clear and should include specific steps to achieve goals as well as methods for measuring success. The final portion dictates whether the child will learn in a general or special education setting and how they will take standardized testing. The following table is an example of what an IEP may look like.

Desired Outcome	Methods/Strategies	Assessment
OCTOBER 2021: **Problem Solving:** Angela will be introduced to different scenarios using methods such as role-play, videos, and stories; and she will be able to verbally describe how to solve a problem three out of four times by next quarter.	Watch videos of school children solving various problems, such as: • Raising their hand to ask to use the restroom. • Writing down and organizing homework assignments. • Packing their backpack with all required supplies before bed. Give immediate feedback as Angela attempts to work out how to solve the problem. Give praise if she answers correctly and redirection if she needs to try a different approach. Have Angela understand different points of view and the expectations of others in each situation. Role-play games can help her place herself in the shoes of another in order to understand the problem more clearly.	FEBRUARY 2022: Angela is progressing and is able to accurately describe steps to solve problems 60% of the time. She is able to determine when she needs assistance, and promptly asks a teacher for help or clarification if she is unsure.

The IEP falls under the Individuals with Disabilities Education Act (IDEA), which ensures access to special education and similar services. Instruction is unique and tailored for the specific needs of the student. Schools determine eligibility for an IEP by considering two main factors: Firstly, does the child have one or more of the 13

EXECUTIVE FUNCTIONING SUPERPOWERS

conditions outlined in the IDEA (listed below), and do they need accommodations and services to succeed in school? The plan is valid through 12th grade but cannot be carried over into college. By law, this document must be updated annually and signed by all parties in attendance at the yearly meeting, including the child if they are in middle or high school. According to Schmidt (2019), the 13 conditions that qualify a student for an IEP are:

1. Autism
2. Deaf-blindness
3. Deafness
4. Emotional disturbance
5. Hearing impairment
6. Learning disability
7. Intellectual disability
8. Multiple disabilities
9. Orthopedic impairment
10. Other health impairment
11. Speech or language impairment
12. Traumatic brain injury
13. Visual impairment

There has been an explosion of knowledge on the topic of executive functioning, particularly among, but not limited to, individuals with diverse ways of thinking, processing, learning, and behaving. As a result, parents, caregivers, and teachers have access to resources unavailable just a few years ago. Information can be found at the click of a mouse, the tap of a finger, or the touch of a screen. This plethora of resources is by no means exhaustive, but it's a great starting point for anyone who suspects that a child is having difficulty with executive functioning skills.

CONCLUSION

Every child is a unique, special, and important person. We all have different abilities, strengths, and weaknesses. No two people are alike, and no method of learning will work for everyone. There is nothing wrong with a child who needs some extra help with their executive functioning skills. After all, every school-aged kid requires guidance in these matters to some extent. Many of the most successful people, with the most powerful minds, experience some issues managing their day-to-day life, and they were often a handful in their early years.

Understanding cause and effect, organizing, planning, and self-monitoring all play an integral role in determining the direction and quality of life. Perfection isn't necessary, needed, or wanted, and all children should understand that. However, introducing these concepts in age-appropriate ways offers the best opportunity for executive functioning skills to come online sooner rather than later.

There's a running joke among parents of very young babies and toddlers that nobody will know when they were potty trained.

There's much humor and truth in that statement. Just like a child who remains in diapers an extra year or two, once executive functioning skills are learned, there is no way to differentiate between kids who learned such behaviors early or late. Childhood is a time of learning with a support system in place, and kids will make mistakes. Life is a never-ending learning experience. By showing that there is no shame in the struggle to achieve, any child can go far.

Executive functioning skills affect every aspect and time of life, from completing book reports to landing a dream job, and everything in between. There is a lot to learn in our bright, modern, and fast-paced world, but not much information on *how* to learn. Following the methods, tools, and techniques discussed in this book is sure to make a difference in the lives of any child, now and in the future. As parents, caregivers, and teachers, it is our responsibility to teach the next generations how to navigate the world as fully functioning adults. Part of growing up is understanding that struggles are a part of life. Nothing comes easily, at least not the things that are worth having. Struggles do not define a person; it's the response to difficulty that proves grit and determination.

Over time, practical application of their executive functioning skills —including flexible thinking, time management, organization, self-awareness, impulse control, working memory, and planning—will ensure children grow into adults who have these positive traits ingrained in their way of life. The leaders of tomorrow will be those who have mastered these behaviors. Don't fret for those who are still on their journey of understanding how to apply these skills to their lives. Those who have a little trouble in the beginning often turn out to be the most successful. Determination and the experience of hard-won change throughout a learning process are facets of a personality that will go far in whatever they put their mind to.

With some attention from their parents and teachers, as well as effort from the kids themselves, children will learn that while their brain may function differently, it's actually a strength that can give them a competitive edge. They can pay attention, plan, stay organized, roll with the changes and follow through, just like all of their favorite superheroes. The process of developing a child's executive functioning superpowers (skills) is fun and exciting; new skills mean more independence. This will be a journey of learning for their caregivers as well. The benefits of developing a child's executive functioning superpowers will be felt both inside and outside the family as children are given the opportunity to grow and flourish in their own unique way.

Thank you so much for purchasing my book, 'Executive Functioning Superpowers.' I hope you found it helpful and informative. If you enjoyed the book and found it valuable, I would be grateful if you could take a few minutes to leave a review. Your review will help others discover the book and decide whether it's right for them.

Thank you for considering leaving a review. I appreciate your feedback and support.

REFERENCES

Balogbog, E. M. (2022). *Bionic reading may be the game changer for neurodivergent readers.* POP! https://pop.inquirer.net/?s=bionic+reading

Beck, C. (2021, May 3). *Self-monitoring strategies for kids.* The OT Toolbox. https://www.theottoolbox.com/self-monitoring-strategies-for-kids/

Bhandari, S. (2004, July). *Nonstimulant therapy and other ADHD drugs.* WebMD. https://www.webmd.com/add-adhd/adhd-nonstimulant-drugs-therapy

Branigan, H., and Kanevski, M. (n.d.). Boosting metacognition and executive functions in the classroom. *The Learning Scientists.* https://www.learningscientists.org/blog/2018/1/9-1

Brookes, P. H. (2018, May 2). 11 tips on breaking tasks down for students: an executive function post. *Brookes Blog.* https://blog.brookespublishing.com/11-tips-on-breaking-tasks-down-for-students-an-executive-function-post/

Brown, T. (2022). *Do kids outgrow executive functioning issues?* Understood.org. https://www.understood.org/articles/en/do-kids-outgrow-executive-functioning-issues

Dawson, P. (2014, December 16). *Improving executive skills.* SmartKidsWithLD. https://www.smartkidswithld.org/getting-help/executive-function-disorder/principles-for-improving-executive-skills/

Delman, M. (n.d.). Self advocacy: Why your child won't seek the teacher's help. *Beyond Book Smart.* Retrieved March 12, 2022, from https://www.beyondbooksmart.com/executive-functioning-strategies-blog/self-advocacy-why-your-child-wont-seek-the-teachers-help

Executive functioning. (2020). Autism Speaks. https://www.autismspeaks.org/executive-functioning

Executive function and self-regulation. (2015). Center on the Developing Child at Harvard University. https://developingchild.harvard.edu/science/key-concepts/executive-function/

Everything for social emotional learning and executive functioning. (2022). Pathway 2 Success. https://www.thepathway2success.com

Fake, C. (2014, September 11). *Memorization, facts and learning to learn.* https://www.google.com/amp/s/caterina.net/2014/09/10/memorization-facts-and-learning-to-learn/amp/

Golden, C., and Tomb, M. (2022). What is a neuropsychological evaluation? Columbia University Department of Psychiatry: Division of Child and Adolescent Psychiatry. https://childadolescentpsych.cumc.columbia.edu/articles/what-neuropsychological-evaluation#what

Hanson, C. (2020). Executive function skills by age: what to look for. *Life Skills Advocate.* https://lifeskillsadvocate.com/blog/executive-function-skills-by-age/#How-Executive-Functioning-Skills-Develop-By-Age

Home. (2022). Tools of the Mind. https://toolsofthemind.org

Home. (2019). George Lucas Educational Foundation. https://www.edutopia.org

Home. (2022). Common Sense Education. https://www.commonsense.org/education

In brief: executive function. (2012). Center on the Developing Child at Harvard University. https://developingchild.harvard.edu/resources/inbrief-executive-function/

Interventions for executive functioning challenges: time management. (2022). The Pathway 2 Success. https://www.thepathway2success.com/interventions-for-executive-functioning-challenges-time-management/

Impulse Control. (2022). Child Mind Institute. https://childmind.org/search/Impulse%20control/

Jacobson, L. A., Williford, A. P., and Pianta, R. C. (2011). The role of executive function in children's competent adjustment to middle school. *Child Neuropsychology,* 17(3), 255–280. https://doi.org/10.1080/09297049.2010.535654

Kelly, K. (2022). *Developmental-behavioral pediatricians: what you need to know.* Understood.org. https://www.understood.org/articles/en/developmental-behavioral-pediatricians-what-you-need-to-know

McIntyre, T. (2022). *Self monitoring of behavior.* Behavior Advisor. http://www.behavioradvisor.com/SelfMonitoring.html

Milne, V. (2020, April 24). *How to know if your kid is struggling with executive functioning skills.* Today's Parent. https://www.todaysparent.com/family/special-needs/executive-functioning-skills/

New Hope Media LLC. (2019). ADDitude Home. https://www.additudemag.com/

Occupational therapists: occupational outlook handbook. (2019, April 10) Bureau of Labor Statistics. https://www.bls.gov/ooh/healthcare/mobile/occupational-therapists.htm

Pietrangelo, A. (2019, December 12). *CBT techniques: tools for cognitive behavioral therapy.* Healthline. https://www.healthline.com/health/cbt-techniques#types-of-cbt-techniques

Pietro, S. (2016, February 26). Helping kids who struggle with executive functions. *Child Mind Institute.* https://childmind.org/article/helping-kids-who-struggle-with-executive-functions/

Rawe, J. (2022). *How to help kids build flexible thinking skills.* Understood.org. https://www.understood.org/articles/en/build-flexible-thinking-child

Resnick, A. (2021). *What is neurodiversity?* Very Well Mind. https://www.verywellmind.com/what-is-neurodiversity-5193463

Rosen, P. (2022). *What is working memory?* Understood.org. https://www.understood.org/articles/en/working-memory-what-it-is-and-how-it-works

Rymanowicz, K. (2016, April 19). *The importance of focus and self-control for young children.* MSU Extension. https://www.canr.msu.edu/news/the_importance_of_focus_and_self_control_for_y-oung_children

Saline, S. (2018, September 26). Learn to scaffold: Build your teen's executive functions all year long. *ADDitude*. https://www.google.-com/amp/s/www.additudemag.com/instructional-scaffolding-executive-functions/amp/

Schmidt, J. (2019, December 27). *IEP or 504 plan: What's best for your student?* N2y. https://www.n2y.com/blog/iep-vs-504-plan/

Simple tips for executive functioning skills in therapy. (2020, June 25). Speechy Musings. https://speechymusings.com/2020/06/25/tips-for-supporting-executive-functioning-skills-in-speech-therapy/

Swetz, H. (2020, October 18). *Executive functioning activities: 50 skill builders for kids of all ages!* The Homeschool Resource Room. https://www.google.com/amp/s/thehomeschoolresourceroom.-com/2020/10/17/executive-functioning-activities/amp/

Stimulant medications for ADHD. (2004, July). WebMD. https://www.webmd.com/add-adhd/adhd-stimulant-therapy#1

Self-monitoring record (universal). (2022). Psychology Tools. https://www.psychologytools.com/resource/self-monitoring-record-universal/

Self-control. (2022). Psychology Today. https://www.google.-com/amp/s/www.psychologytoday.com/us/basics/self-control%3famp

The world's leading website on learning disabilities and ADHD. (2019). LDonline. http://www.ldonline.org

Todo telling time. (2013). Edshelf. https://edshelf.com/tool/todo-telling-time/

Understood Team. (2022a). *A day in the life of a child with executive functioning issues.* Understood. https://www.understood.org/articles/en/a-day-in-the-life-of-a-child-with-executive-functioning-issues

Understood Team. (2022b). *What is self-control?* Understood. https://www.understood.org/articles/en/self-control-what-it-means-for-kids

Villines, Z. (2019, June 6). Executive function disorder: symptoms, causes, and treatment. *Medical News Today.* https://www.medical-newstoday.com/articles/325402#causes

Wiki Targeted Entertainment. (2022). *Skills and abilities.* Superhero Wiki. https://superheroes.fandom.com/wiki/Skills_and_Abilities

Wilson, D. M., and Gross, D. (2018). Parents' executive functioning and involvement in their child's education: an integrated literature review. *Journal of School Health*, 88(4), 322–329. https://doi.org/10.1111/josh.12612

Wright, L. (2022). *8 fun games that can improve your child's executive functioning skills.* Understood. https://www.understood.org/articles/en/8-fun-games-that-can-improve-your-childs-executive-functioning-skills

What is autonomy supportive parenting? (2021, July 15). Bright Horizons. https://www.brighthorizons.com/family-resources/autonomy-supported-parenting

ACKNOWLEDGMENTS

I would like to express my deepest gratitude to all those who have supported me in the creation of my book, *Executive Functioning Superpowers*.

I am incredibly grateful to my family and friends who provided encouragement, motivation, and inspiration as I worked on this project. Your belief in my abilities and your unwavering support meant the world to me.

I would also like to extend a heartfelt thank you to Mads Johan Øgaard for creating the stunning cover art for my book. His talent and creativity brought my vision to life.

Thank you all for being a part of this journey.

ABOUT THE AUTHOR

Máire Powell is an experienced social worker with over twenty years of practice in working with children, adolescents, and adults. She is particularly interested in neurodiverse conditions that impact executive functioning. As a result, Máire Powell is well-equipped to address the unique needs of young people struggling with executive functioning skills. In addition, her extensive knowledge and experience in both educational and home settings have allowed her to identify and support the potential in individuals with executive functioning struggles. In her book *Executive Functioning Superpowers,* she offers parents, teachers, and professionals the tools and strategies to support and empower children to reach their full potential.

For more information check out mairepowell.com

 facebook.com/MaireEFS

Made in the USA
Las Vegas, NV
06 October 2023

78695356R00098